THE GRADUATE GRIND

CRITICAL EDUCATION PRACTICE
VOLUME 20

THE GRADUATE GRIND
A CRITICAL LOOK AT GRADUATE EDUCATION

PATRICIA HINCHEY
ISABEL KIMMEL

NEW YORK AND LONDON

First published by Falmer Press
This edition published 2013 by Routledge
711 Third Avenue, New York, NY 10017
2 Park Square, Milton Park, Abingdon, Oxon, OX14 4RN
Routledge is an imprint of the Taylor & Francis Group, an informa business

Copyright © 2000 by Patricia Hinchey and Isabel Kimmel

All rights reserved. No part of this book may be reprinted or reproduced or utilized in any form or by any electronic, mechanical, or other means, now known or hereafter invented, including photocopying and recording, or in any information storage or retrieval system, without permission in writing from the publisher.

10 9 8 7 6 5 4 3 2 1

Library of Congress Cataloging-in-Publication Data
Library of Congress Cataloging-in-Publication Data is available from the Library of Congress.

Hinchey, Patricia and Isabel Kimmel
The graduate grind : a critical look at graduate education / Particia Hinchey and Isabel Kimmel.
p. cm.—(Garland reference library of social science ; v. 1421 Critical education practice ; v. 20)
Includes bibliographical references and index.
ISBN 0-8153-3397-8 (alk. paper) — ISBN 0-8153-3835-X (pbk. : alk. paper)

Between the time Website information is gathered and date of publication, individual sites may have moved or may no longer be active. Therefore, the publisher cannot guarantee thet the Websites listed herein are still accessible at the URL provided.

Contents

Acknowledgments		vii
Preface		ix
Chapter 1	Problems and Perspectives	1
	Questioning Trends in Graduate Education	1
	Defining "The Problem"	3
Chapter 2	Sources of Institutional Power: Constructed Consciousness, Hegemony, and Reification	25
	Constructed Consciousness: Lessons from Experience	26
	Institutional Hegemony: Graduate Student Perception of Place and Power	35
	Reification: Institutions That Can Do No Wrong	40
Chapter 3	Institutional Cultures and Power: The Minefield of Conflicting Identities	45
	The Influence of Culture on Behavior	45
	Culture as an Interpretive Lens	46
	Institutional Cultures and Student Experience	61
Chapter 4	Culture and Oppression: The "Other" as Graduate Student	63
	Forms of Oppression	65
	Experience of the Other	69
	Realities	88

Chapter 5	Power and the Dissertation: Faculty as Demigods	89
	Ritual and Gatekeeping	89
	Dilemmas and Demigods	93
Chapter 6	Voices of the Oppressed	109
Chapter 7	How Might Things Be Otherwise?	135
	Recent Thoughts on Reform	137
	Consensus on Practical Concerns	138
	Philosophical Concerns	150
	Parting Thoughts	163
	References	165
	Index	171

Acknowledgments

For inspiration and support, we are sincerely grateful to Joe Kincheloe, Shirley Steinberg, Bobbi and Scott Kerlin, Rick Weibl, our writing friends, and the many who have challenged and energized our thinking in recent years. For practical support, we owe hours of time and endless gratitude to our on-call librarian, Eloise Bartosh, and to our on-call word-processing wonder, Lynne Fazio. For their trust and their stories, we thank the many graduate students who took the time to contribute to this work. For tough and loving editing, we thank Judith Rae Davis and Melanie Morgon. And for the nurturing partnerships that enable everything we do, we thank Joe Kimmel and Ed Hinchey.

Preface

In Shirley's Jackson's classic short story "The Lottery," much that strikes the reader as absurd constitutes unquestioned, routine reality for the story's characters. Why does the annual lottery occur? Because it's been in place longer than anyone can remember; it's a tradition that's been in place for so long it has become reified. Faced with the possibility of sacrificing her own life as a result of a town lottery, a mother lobbies to include the names of her own daughter and son-in-law among those at risk in order to increase her own chances of survival. In the moment of acting out what tradition requires of them as a result of a random drawing, the townspeople eventually stone to death a living breathing human being they had formerly greeted warmly as neighbor, wife, mother, friend.

Jackson's story provokes the reader to question the extent to which a society can incorporate absurdity into accepted ritual, despite a high price in terms of humanity. If we question graduate school rituals in the way she suggests, parallels between Jackson's fictional world and the world of graduate education become evident—and frightening. Survival rituals (meeting purposeless requirements, passing meaningless tests) exist long past a time when the rationale for this or that practice has faded from institutional memory. The need to survive a graduate program forces students to abandon any impulse to generosity or collaboration and to adopt instead a hard, self-protective demeanor. If survival can come only at the expense of others—so be it.

Having earned doctorates, which means having experienced the effect of the graduate school rituals upon our own habits and humanity, we became alarmed by the impact of unquestioned practice on the people who, like Jackson's townspeople, live out time-honored routines they've inherited. What practices determine who will be given power and who will suffer its abuses? Are allocation practices fair, just, humane—or even sensible? Once assigned, how is power used? What is the effect of power on both those who have it and those who don't? What kind of society does the prevailing power structure create in the academic world of graduate school? What kind of society are graduates prepared to create when they leave the school with a degree in hand?

This text explores those questions from the perspective of critical theory, which asks always who has the power, how they acquire and use it, and how various constituencies are affected by existing arrangements. We've gathered together narratives of the graduate school townspeople—the stories of graduate students themselves—and we've probed them to uncover the power structure that provided the stage for their experience. We've developed some hypotheses in response to the questions that prompted this study. And, certainly, we've formed strong attitudes along the way.

We hope this text will help you do the same.

The Graduate Grind

CHAPTER 1
Problems and Perspectives

> *To stay in touch with the educational needs of an increasingly nontraditional clientele, habit must give way to invention. Before innovation can occur, however, we must systematically disassemble the machinery and defects of the old order so that a new one may be erected.*
> —W.T. QUINNAN

QUESTIONING TRENDS IN GRADUATE EDUCATION

In late August 1978, a doctoral student at Stanford walked into his advisor's office and bludgeoned the professor to death with four blows to the head, after years of considering the "bloody plan." Later, he commented:

> "Stanford, with [this professor's] help, took nineteen years of my life with impunity and I decided I would not let that pass. I decided I'd do something about it. I did. Under the same circumstances, I'd do it again." (Cude 1987, 45)

Nearly two decades later, in August 1996, a masters student at the University of San Diego entered the room where he was to defend his masters thesis and, before the defense began, shot his three professors dead. Just two years later, in August 1998, a promising graduate student at Harvard committed suicide—only a year after another student in the same department also took his own life (Hall 1998).

Though such murderous events continue to shock outsiders, experienced insiders have less reason for surprise: the culture of graduate study is rife with metaphors reflecting doctoral study as a perilous—a downright dangerous—enterprise. In literature for and about graduate students, the word *survival* is a staple in such typical titles as *How to Complete and Survive a Doctoral Dissertation* (Sternberg 1981); *Survival of the Fittest* (S.P. Kerlin 1995); *A Woman's Guide to Surviving in the Academic World* (Caplan 1994); and *High Noon: Surviving the*

Comprehensive Exams (McConnell 1982). At least one writer suggests that survival of higher education in general is possible only by killing off at least some part of oneself in the process: *Killing the Spirit: Higher Education in America* (Smith 1990). Such was precisely the experience Jane Tompkins reports:

> When I talk about graduate school, try as I may, I can't keep the bitterness from creeping into my voice. Though my idealism about literature was partly based on ignorance and snobbery and self-protectiveness, it was real nevertheless. It was an expression of love and the best thing I had to offer. At Yale I spent five years learning how to strangle my love, and I never quite got over it. (1996, 76–77)

With all this killing, dying, and surviving, it's no wonder that stress is a given during the process, as is evident in research studies with such titles as *New Brains for Old Bodies: The Impact of Emotional and Physical Stress During the Ph.D. Process* (Barnett 1982) and *Student "Burnout" as a Mediator of the Stress–Outcome Relationship* (Koeske & Koeske 1991). Psychologists talk about "trauma" associated with doctoral study (Bowen & Rudenstine 1992, 2); one article reports on *Doctoral Disorder of Adulthood* (Dooley-Dickey & Satcher 1991), and—despite its references to doctoral candidates wearing lucky underwear to committee meetings—it's difficult to determine whether the article is satire or not. One extensive study of female graduate students finds that terms they use to describe their experiences typically include "loneliness, isolation, exhaustion, stress, anxiety, hazing, ridicule, sexual harassment, benign neglect and even abuse" (B. Kerlin 1995, 35).

Even if the student survives such strain, relationships may not. Academic observers and commentators note frequent marital and family stress in articles with such subheads and titles as *Does Academic Life Lead to Divorce?* (Boufis 1999) and *The Impossible Dream: The Ph.D, Marriage, and Family* (Levstik 1982). Faculty mentors once considered good friends are pictured as potential foes in pieces like *Doctoral Advisement Relationships Between Women: On Friendship and Betrayal* (Heinrich 1995).

With so many hardships, it's hardly surprising that it takes all students years, and many students years and years and years, to complete the undertaking. Hawley summarizes a 1990 report that shows the average time-to-degree, including periods when students were not formally registered, varied from 7.6 years for physical science students to 18 years for education students—quite an extended period of suffering and trying to survive (1993, 16). Many students don't. Indeed, so many students leave even after reaching dissertation phase that the phenomenon has spawned its own degree-echoing abbreviation: ABD (all but dissertation). Surveying recent research in graduate study, Bowen and Rudenstine note that

> only about half of all entering students in many Ph.D. programs eventually obtain doctorates (frequently after pursuing degrees anywhere from six to twelve years). In sharp contrast, it is common for completion rates in leading professional schools of business, law, and medicine to exceed 90 percent. And it is not just the plight of the ABDs . . . that has caused completion rates in Ph.D. programs to be low; attrition has been high at all stages of graduate study. Moreover, attrition appears to have increased over the last three decades. (1992, 105)

These authors further report that one study of both large and smaller programs found that of students who returned for a second year of graduate study, some 30 percent never achieved ABD status and of those who did, more than 25 percent never completed dissertations and doctorates (p. 253). So: one out of every three students who remain in a program after the first year leaves without ABD status; of the original 50 percent of entering students who do become ABDs, one in every four will never complete the doctorate. And, the number of graduate students overall who abandon doctoral programs has been increasing for over thirty years.

The literature overflows with documented emotional stress and student breaking points, including even murder, as in the case of the Stanford student, who was provoked to such violence, to his murderous breaking point, by an unsurprising but debilitating series of common graduate school experiences, including "inch[ing] through his doctoral program as his marriage collapsed and his debts accumulated, [and] . . . years in which each academic hurdle he surmounted led only to another . . . years in which his discouragement, frustration and desperation smoldered toward violent expression" (Cude 1987, 46). Suicide. Divorce. Burnout. Betrayal. All duly noted—even somewhat expected and accepted—outcomes. What's going on here? Does anyone even see a problem? And, even if they do, does anyone care?

DEFINING "THE PROBLEM"

The answer to the question "What's going on here?"—as is true just about everywhere else—depends on who is answering the question.

Every researcher knows that much depends on the way a problem is defined, and every honest researcher also knows that problem definition is itself shaped in large measure by the interests and proclivities of the particular person who happens to be doing the research. Asking whether there's a safety problem in the auto industry, for example, might easily result in at least two different versions of the problem. An industrial group might answer: "Yes, there certainly is a problem: regulatory agencies are imposing increasing and unreasonable safety standards that will reduce our profits to a level unacceptable to our stockholders." However, a consumer safety group might respond to the same question with a starkly contrasting problem definition: "Yes, there certainly is a problem: consumer safety is being callously sacrificed on the altar of corporate greed and causing thousands of needless deaths every year." Two groups may easily be able to agree that a problem exists, yet unable to agree on its nature.

Such is the case in graduate education. Recently there's been some talk about reform—but the questions of why reform might be necessary, and what kind is needed, is an area open to wide interpretation.

Institutional Perspective: The AAU Report, 1998

There is evidence that organizations with a stake in graduate education are beginning to openly explore the question of whether there are problems in the enterprise. Not surprisingly, answers forthcoming from university representatives have at their heart a variety of self-interests, with the lived experience of graduate students a peripheral concern at best.

A 1998 report from the American Association of Universities (AAU) is a case in point. The association considers itself "an appropriate organization to examine the state of graduate education" because, although its member universities comprise only 16 percent of America's Ph.D.-granting universities, they produce over 50 percent of the country's Ph.D.s (1998a, 6). Moreover, AAU institutions account for 93 percent of those appearing in top ten disciplinary rankings released in 1996 by the National Research Council. With these credentials, it formed a Committee on Graduate Education comprised of "university presidents, chief academic officers, and graduate deans" whose responsibility was to "examine current problems, identify evolving needs, and policy changes [sic]" (1998a, 6).

The resulting report, AAU's *Report and Recommendations,* traces its origin to growing criticism of graduate education, and claims to be evidence that academe is taking criticism seriously. The executive summary notes that specific criticisms have included "overproduction of Ph.D.s; narrow training; emphasis on research over teaching; use of students to meet institutional needs at the expense of sound education; and insufficient mentoring, career advising, and job placement assistance" (1998a, 1). The important and recurring charge of student exploitation—the "use of students to meet institutional needs at the expense of a sound education"—is reiterated in the body of the report:

> The view emerging from . . . national and institutional examinations of graduate education is that the balance between institutional and departmental benefits from and responsibilities for graduate education has in many cases shifted too far in the direction of institutional and departmental benefits, to the detriment of graduate students and programs. (1998a, 17)

This reiteration is followed immediately by the claim that "Concerted efforts should be and have been made to right this balance" (17). However, the report offers little substantive detail and evidence to support that claim, with the single exception of the "Preparing Future Faculty" program (discussed in Chapter 7).

Whatever the details of efforts to alleviate student exploitation, it seems safe to infer that this area remains a problem. In fact, the section "Institutional Responsibilities for Graduate Education" begins with this paragraph:

> The overriding purpose of graduate education is and must always be the education of graduate students. In designing graduate programs and advising graduate students, university administrators and faculty members must hold the interests of students paramount. (1998a, 14)

The section then notes that "Graduate students learn to teach and to conduct research by performing these activities under faculty mentorship" (14). The claim here is that the work graduate students do for the institution is a sort of internship from which they learn to teach and research effectively. In this way, the report justifies providing financial support through teaching or research assistantships as being in the students' own interest, a way to learn important professional skills.

This is a traditional, and reasonable, argument which would be more credible if the report's best practices guidelines addressed the problem that the report itself warns against: "if student interests become subsidiary to conflicting institutional or faculty interests, the educational benefits of these apprenticeship arrangements can be undermined" (1998a, 15). Pressuring graduate students into time-consuming teaching or research assistantships slows progress to degree—but it also offers the university an endless supply of cheap labor, which is why the problem of exploitation has become increasingly serious. What safeguards does the AAU report offer as "best practice" to end such exploitation?

Although the report offers some twenty specific recommendations in eight different categories, only one speaks directly to protecting students from exploitation. This timidly worded suggestion is found under "Financial Support":

> Financial support should be designed to assist students in their progress to a degree; financial support through work that draws students away from their graduate programs should be avoided. (1998a, 3)

However, the section on "External Support for Graduate Education" contains this suggestion:

> States support graduate education primarily through teaching and research assistantships at resident public universities. (1998a, 5)

How are students to be protected from work that slows their progress if funding continues to remain heavily in the form of teaching and research assistantships? Why not more grants or scholarships? It is difficult, at best, to reconcile the recommendation that institutions should avoid "financial support through work that draws students away from their graduate programs" with the recommendation that primary funding from states take the form of teaching and research assistantships.

These suggestions seem contradictory, and only two others seem related in any way to the exploitation issue: one that recommends institutions provide data on institutional completion rates and time-to-degree to all applicants, and one that recommends institutions compare department program performance against the program's own articulated goals and expectations. A paraphrase of these points taken together might read: "Institutions must ensure that student interests always come first, and it's evident that assistantships can undermine a student's education. Therefore, institutions should reveal their stance on exploitation to applicants by providing statistics on completion rates and average time-to-degree.

That way, the buyers can beware. As long as students are fairly warned and have an opportunity to shop around, institutions can continue to promote research and teaching assistantships, maintaining their supply of cheap labor."

This discrepancy between professed principles and recommended actions undermines the AAU's claim to be taking criticisms seriously, and statements from another AAU document make that claim downright incredible. As noted above, the AAU defends research and teaching assistantships as a way for graduate students to learn the skills they will need as professionals. But another AAU document, *Graduate Education in the National Interest,* characterizes graduate students far differently than novices honing new skills:

> Graduate education benefits the institutions in which it is carried out. . . . Graduate students, closer in age and cultural experience to undergraduate students than faculty members, may be able to find the crucial connections that will make subjects come alive and spark a lifelong interest in a particular discipline. The vitality and creativity of bright, young students working in a research lab can invigorate a research program and launch new lines of inquiry. . . . Graduate students function as connecting links in the modern research university, bringing faculty together from across disciplinary units for student-initiated conferences and workshops, as well as on dissertation committees. (1998b, 9)

The *Report* document asserts that graduate students must learn to teach and conduct research via assistantships, but this document characterizes them as teaching more inspirationally than regular faculty, sparking new lines of thought for entrenched researchers, and charting new interdisciplinary territory (1998a). Inspired teaching and research are what we'd expect from already skilled faculty members, but *Graduate Education in the National Interest* suggests that graduate students outperform experienced faculty in important ways. The AAU can't have it both ways: either graduate students are novices who need assistantships to learn professional skills, or they are skilled scholars contributing immeasurably to the work of the university—at bargain basement rates. To be credible, the AAU's arguments must be much more consistent.

For all the rhetoric about the need to serve student interests first, there is little in the AAU report to suggest that its interest in graduate study hinges on student welfare. In fact, much suggests that institutional concern is more genuinely a concern about finance. In general, universities, proud of maintaining tradition and of housing competing ideologies, are not known for being sensitive to outside criticism—unless it comes from a major source of income like the federal government or a state legislature. In the case of graduate education, significant loss of income is a real threat, and, in general, both the 1998 report and *Graduate Education in the National Interest* offer evidence that finance is institutions' genuine concern. High levels of attrition and an uncharacteristic drop in enrollment threatening institutional revenue are two factors that have sparked the AAU's interest:

> Students clearly are responding to the perceived market. A recent survey by the Council of Graduate Schools and the Graduate Record Examinations Board found that overall graduate enrollments in 1996 dropped for the first time in 10 years, although with considerable variability among the disciplines. In addition to decisions by some universities to scale back their programs, this decline is attributed to a strong labor market for new bachelor's degree recipients, increased opportunities for foreign students in their home countries, and student concerns about the reported excess of Ph.D.s. (1998b, 2)

This drop in enrollment means a loss of tuition dollars, although that is perhaps the least of universities' financial worries. The other is the frightening possibility of decreased federal funding. The report frets:

> First-rate graduate education is expensive, and both universities and the federal government have raised questions about how—and at what level—it should be funded ... Understandably, federal agencies try to stretch their dollars as far as they can ... Occasionally federal agencies try to reduce their contribution to the costs of graduate education in the hope that either students themselves or the universities will make up the difference. But graduate students already have foregone other forms of employment and may be burdened with substantial debt. Universities are hard pressed to make the contributions beyond the considerable investments they already make to graduate education. (1998b, 1–2)

How much money is at stake here? Vast sums. According to the *Report*, the federal government "invested $171 billion in research and development (R&D) in 1995" (1998a, 6).

The amount of money invested by the federal government explains why it has been interested in evaluating the performance of graduate education with an eye to identifying problems, especially in light of scandals that uncovered federal money being misappropriated to fund such items as housing for university officers (Grassmuck 1991; M. Anderson 1996). Federal interest in potential problems, like institutional interest, is rooted in concern for a "bottom line." Is there a desirable cost-benefit ratio in graduate study? For example, do federally underwritten and particularly expensive programs enroll enough students to justify their cost? Are candidates being credentialed in areas where employers need them, or is there a glut in one area and a shortage in another? While employability is surely a concern for students, it is investors' return on their dollars rather than student welfare that seems the heart of institutional reports.

The rhetoric of sections like the following amplifies the meaning of the title *Graduate Education in the National Interest* and clarifies exactly where official interest lies:

> Just as federal investment in basic research serves the nation by filling a crucial gap that neither states nor industry will fill, federal investment in graduate education serves the same essential role. Talented students who receive graduate degrees are a highly mobile national resource. States, therefore, often are reluctant to invest in graduate education fellowships. Similarly, industry investment in graduate fellowships is difficult to justify since a company cannot be sure that it, rather than a competitor, will receive the dividends from the investment. When the federal government makes the investment, the nation reaps the dividends regardless of where the recipient of the fellowship ends up working. (1998b, 1–2)

The focus here is not on students and student interest, but on graduates as potential resources in service to the national economy. This perspective embodies human capital theory, which Schied says "basically holds that long-term benefits or rate of return from an individual's investment in education are superior to other forms of investment" (Schied 1995) and that education "increases the skills and thence the productivity of the workforce" (4). The concern of the investors is so far away from the welfare of the recipients that Schied titles his piece *How Did Humans Become Resources Anyway?*—an apparent effort to remind readers that there is a difference between a human being and a barrel of oil. We might ask a similar question about graduate students: how did they become national economic resources rather than colleagues and apprentices?

And exactly what sort of resources are they to be? Whose needs will they fill? The report answers:

> Graduate education prepares the scientists and engineers needed by industry, government, and universities to conduct the nation's research and development; educates the scholars in the humanities, social sciences, and the arts who preserve and enlarge our understanding of human thought and the human condition; and develops the scholars in all disciplines who become the faculty of the nation's colleges and universities. (1998a, 2)

Graduate education is important because it provides credentialed manpower to serve national needs: research and development for a healthy economy; preservation and enrichment of our cultural heritage. And all of this is in addition to the low-cost teaching and research services the students provide to the university during their doctoral programs.

Despite the frequent refrain that graduate programs must serve student needs first, much in the AAU documents undermines that claim by repeatedly discussing the many ways graduate students function as resources to serve the needs of institutions, the needs of the labor market, and the needs of society. Like the car manufacturer who loudly assures the public that safety is a high priority and that he sincerely regrets people being killed in unsafe vehicles, the report repeatedly asserts a commitment to student welfare and condemns student exploitation. Yet, just as car manufacturers often stall to avoid costly recalls of unsafe vehicles, the AAU avoids endorsing any costly recommendation that might significantly alleviate student exploitation. It is not wrong to acknowledge that graduate students are resources. What is wrong is to exploit them shamelessly while loudly proclaiming that student welfare is an overarching concern to institutions.

In addition to its contradictory recommendations about assistantships, the report's recommendations include other examples of doublespeak that undermine credibility. For example, while an earlier section of the report criticizes federal policy for insisting that research assistants working on federally funded projects must be classified as employees (1998a, 17), the following recommendation, at best, waffles on the student vs. employee question:

> Financial support should be designed to assist students in their progress to a degree. To the extent possible, this support should not involve work that draws students away from their graduate programs. In

Problems and Perspectives

particular, students should not be supported as teaching and research assistants without progressing to greater levels of responsibility and independence; students supported primarily to meet the teaching needs of departments or institutions, or the research needs of faculty research projects, should be reclassified and compensated appropriately. (1998a, 24)

In other words, institutions shouldn't offer financial "support" that will delay students' own academic progress—unless they deem such exploitation necessary. In that case, it's acceptable to put students to work in jobs that will undermine their own progress as long as certain conditions are met: The institution should make the jobs of more experienced TAs or RAs a bit different than the jobs of new ones; pay overworked student-employees a little better; and give them different titles. It will still take them longer to earn a degree, of course, but the institution might incur a little less criticism for its actions. Again, it is hard to reconcile the AAU refrain that students' best interests must guide educational policies with its detailed guidelines for how to structure and compensate work that will delay student progress.

This discussion of how to classify and compensate students appropriately when their work supports not their education but someone else's agenda also seems at odds with the report's earlier claim that federal regulations insisting that research assistants be designated as employees run "counter to sound educational policy" (1998b, 18). How can it be inappropriate for the federal government to term research assistants "employees" when the AAU suggests that if they are treated primarily as workers rather than students, they should be "reclassified and compensated accordingly"?

Here's another murky example dealing with financial issues:

All admitted students should be given accurate information about the costs they will incur and realistic assessments of future prospects for financial support; to the extent possible, these students should be assured of multiyear financial support. (1998a, 24)

Since tuition fees are published and readily accessible, one can only speculate about what this recommendation to give "accurate" information actually means. Is the report urging disclosure about purposefully hidden costs, like tuition for required courses taught only in summer (by faculty who are paid handsome stipends for this "extra" teaching) or tuition for "doctoral advisement" even when the student is 1,000 miles away from the institution and/or the advisor is on sabbatical or out of the country for a semester? Moreover, how is the institution to be realistic in discussing what new sources of revenue might be available to students and which sources might (or might not) offer them additional funds at some unspecified future time? Or does this recommendation simply mean that if there's no chance of future funding, the university should just say so? This suggestion sounds suspiciously like a suggestion that institutions begin embracing honesty—implying a sad commentary on how affairs in higher education are currently being conducted.

Even when doublespeak doesn't come into play, the report's soft shoe around one of the most scandalous elements of graduate education—irresponsible and unprofessional faculty advising (which will be discussed in detail in Chapter 6)—undermines the report's credibility. The two recommendations related to faculty mentoring, which has been criticized as "insufficient," suggest that faculty should confer with students "on a frequent basis" and should provide the department with "periodic" assessments on student progress (1998a, 24). No guidelines for frequency; no suggestion that protective guidelines be put in place; no suggestion on policy offering recourse for wronged students; just a gentle nudge to try to do better.

In short, to appear to be taking criticisms seriously, the recommendations suggest that all institutions "should" do whatever they can to alleviate exploitation. To counter criticism, the report has presented a list of recent initiatives which appear to demonstrate good faith. But how can readers take much reassurance from these good intentions and sample reform strategies? Probably as reassured as we are when CEOs in any other major industry—automobile or tobacco, for example—tell us that they are doing all they *can* do about consumer safety and they are fully aware of the kinds of things they *should* be doing and will *try* to do better.

This may appear to be an overly cynical analysis of a report that does focus on legitimate issues and constitutes some effort on the part of academe to acknowledge and address current problems. But given the blatantly self-interested context of much of the text, given the report's resistance to honest discussion of legitimate criticism from students and others interested in the quality of the doctoral experience, and given the recommendations' consistent refrain that institutions should comply *if* they think compliance is feasible, it's difficult to be enthusiastic about this much publicized document.

Whatever the reader may think of the report, however, it does consti-

Problems and Perspectives 13

tute a representative institutional answer to the question "Is there a problem in graduate education?" Yes. The report finds that growing public criticism and declining enrollment threaten university reputation and funding, a situation that can harm not only the health of the institutions but also that of the nation. The health and welfare of students, however, are not integral to this diagnosis.

An Evolving Focus on Student Experience

Whereas the AAU report is typical in its nearly exclusive focus on finances, statistics, and human resources, a growing number of studies that start with the same numbers move past them into other areas often related to *quality* of graduate students' lived experience. Melissa Anderson captures this evolving perspective in her introduction to a recent collection of essays based on "student experiences from firsthand data of one kind or another":

> Graduate faculties, specialized instruction, research facilities, libraries, and other resources are all expensive. Not surprisingly, most of what is written about graduate education has to do with federal and other investments, supply and demand in academic and professional labor markets, and programs of advanced instruction and research.
> But what of the students themselves? (1998, 1)

This is a question evident in a growing body of research.

In a major and widely cited study, for example, Bowen and Rudenstine define current conditions as problematic in both practical and ethical terms:

> Recognition of the extraordinary amounts of time and effort (as well as money) that many of the brightest students are expected to invest in graduate study heightens still more the feeling that it is wrong simply to accept the current rates of attrition and present assumptions about how long it should take to earn a doctorate. (1992, 3)

Here, research is based on a need to explore criticisms honestly not only because they can hurt the university and country, but also because universities have a responsibility to offer *students* the best possible return on *their* investment in graduate study.

Unlike the AAU report—and not surprisingly, given that researchers who acknowledge students as stakeholders define the problem with a broader perspective than institutional representatives—such studies often arrive at recommendations that seem to serve student welfare at some expense to the university. Bowen and Rudenstine, for example, uncover a factor that has a demonstrable impact on time-to-degree but is not explicitly acknowledged in the AAU report:

> Graduate programs with relatively small entering cohorts have had consistently higher completion rates and lower time-to-degree than those with larger entering cohorts. Limiting the analysis to recipients of national fellowships demonstrates that associated differences in the selectivity of students and provision of financial aid do not eliminate these differentials. (1992, 12)

If institutions genuinely want to shorten time-to-degree, then cutting back on large programs seems a viable strategy. However, such cuts might cost universities both tuition fees and reputation—although they would certainly alleviate an experiential problem *for students* that Smith refers to as "the disease of giantism":

> True learning is clearly incompatible with immensity. Formalism, lifeless routines, bureaucratic obtuseness, coldness of heart, and impoverishment of spirit are the inevitable consequences of excessive size. (1990, 179)

From this perspective, problems in the graduate enterprise include its academic, emotional, and spiritual impact on human students who are not just one of many national economic resources, but *people* with minds and hearts and souls.

Perhaps no researchers have paid more attention to students' lived experience of graduate school or have better cast it as problematic than Scott Kerlin (1994, 1995a, 1995b) and Bobbi Kerlin (1994, 1995, 1997, 1998). Aligning themselves with other researchers who have called for studies on how students themselves perceive their experiences (Tinto 1993; Lipschutz 1993), the Kerlins have been collecting and analyzing narratives from students for several years, trying to better understand how, and for whom, the process is problematic and with what consequences. In their own words, such work

> attempts to mediate between two silences (LeCompte 1993)—the silence 'within', in which participants examine and give voice to their

Problems and Perspectives 15

> own thinking and understanding of their doctoral experience and the meaning this holds for them within the larger context of their own lives—and the silence 'without': the silence between those groups for whom there exists a differential relationship of power. This study seeks to make visible the inner silence of the graduate experience to those in positions of power who might otherwise not see or know these student voices. (S. Kerlin & B. Smith 1994, 19)

Such contributions are essential to genuine understanding of current conditions, because conversation about the status quo will be unavoidably ill informed if students are silenced. A close look at the results of the Kerlins' research makes painfully obvious the kind of information about graduate study that has been excluded to date.

Scott Kerlin's work urges researchers to ask questions like these:

> [W]hat does pursuit of the doctorate mean to today's students? What expectations and hopes do doctoral students carry into the educational process, and what personal feelings result from having pursued the doctorate? Do most doctoral recipients emerge from their educational experiences with greater feelings of "worth," "intelligence," and "ability"?
>
> And what about students who begin but do not complete the doctorate? Does non-completion have lasting negative consequences for students? Are some students more likely to withdraw before finishing, and why? (1995a, 3)

When students speak to such issues in Scott Kerlin's work, their voices reveal a perspective on dollars-and-cents that is worlds away from that of the institutional obsession with its own "bottom line." Consider, for example, this response from a 1994 Ph.D. concerning how graduate education affected his "financial circumstances":

> As for financial circumstances, it's fortunate that financial considerations aren't a high priority for me, since the impact there has clearly been large and negative. I've never added this up before, so this should be interesting. Let's see, the year before I returned to school, my earnings were approximately $42,000. Add 7 years of inflation (assuming no major promotions, and investment income limited to the rate of inflation), and that's about $55,000 in 1993 dollars, times 8 years in school is $440,000. Instead, my actual earnings plus fellowship support over the last 8 years totalled about $90,000 in current dollars, for a loss of $350,000. Add another $15,000 in tuition costs and we're up to

> $365,000. Now suppose I take an assistant prof position at $35,000. That's $20,000 less than $55,000. If we assume the lag remains fairly constant, I would lose another $20,000 for every year I work. So I'm already down by $365,000, and if I retire at 65, that'd be another $620,000, for a grand total of $985,000. Damn, just missed a million. Clearly one does not go to grad school to get rich. (1995b, 21)

It's unlikely, at best, that a dean or chief institutional officer would think to imagine constraints on student support in such personal terms, and the real financial problem—for universities and students both—becomes clarified only when each of these disparate perspectives is considered.

Other comments touch on topics that are routinely excluded from much existing research and that are far less wryly amusing:

> I came into graduate school with the expectation of finding a faculty position. But I don't want to be on a faculty now because I don't have any patience with the endless, non-productive meetings or with perpetuating a practice that is outdated and unresponsive to the needs of the population it serves. I've been here long enough to see that junior faculty members come in with the best of intentions about not following "the format" but the cultural pressure is too much to go up against and in the end, conformity occurs (along with disenchantment). I do know that not all departments are like this, but I think it is the norm. . . . Although economic hardship has been a major challenge, for me the most difficult challenge has been to be thrust into the role of 'suppliant' to those whose teaching and scholarship is in contrast to stated values of the program. Another very difficult challenge has been the racism and classism from my 'educated' professors. (1995b, 24–25)

When the problem of faculty mentoring—given scant attention in the AAU report—is presented from this intensely personal perspective, again the topic takes on a new, and much more urgent, meaning.

Bobbi Kerlin's work centers more particularly on women. In it, many women give voice to the challenges, obstacles, and threats that imperil their success, as well as their physical, emotional, and mental health. Again, simply hearing the female students' voices focuses issues in an entirely new way:

> The department seemed so cold. And the message I started getting very early was that if one is to be a researcher that is what one must be—that

there is little room in one's life for outside commitments in the form of family and relationships (ones that lasted anyway!). (1995, 23)

In many doctoral programs, women soon learn that many academics consider the options of becoming a researcher and of having a family mutually exclusive. Practical policy often reinforces this mindset, as this former graduate student notes:

... there are no provisions for maternity/paternity leave for RA/TA graduate students working for the university. To gain 6 weeks of leave time, I worked double-time the quarter before I had my first child. (B. Kerlin 1995, 23)

A woman who doesn't heed this message can find herself in academic difficulty very quickly:

Several faculty members in my department said that female graduate students who decide to have children while in graduate school are often thought by the department to not be "dedicated" to their research.... My husband was told (by his advisor, and at least one other faculty member) that any woman who got pregnant while in the graduate program before their dissertation proposal meeting would be considered "undedicated" and removed from the program. Essentially, they would not "pass" the dissertation proposal, and would not be allowed to make revisions. He was told that if a student tried to challenge it, the department would simply say the student didn't meet their academic requirements. He was also told that it was OK for men to have children, provided that it didn't interfere with their "duties" in the department. (B. Kerlin 1995, 24)

For students who take heed and avoid becoming involved with their own families, few other options may appear for human company and support:

Most of the students themselves were so consumed with concerns of continued funding and "competing" with one another for these scarce resources that few relationships were formed. And, those that were formed tended to align themselves along faculty interests so, there was at all times an inherent division among the students based upon this. (B. Kerlin 1995, 33)

The rules of the game, the competitive climate, and the constant focus on survival leave many students bitter about their "education":

> The graduate experience, all six years of it, felt much more like a fraternity hazing than an educational experience. I got very tired of constantly being asked to "prove" my worth to faculty and fellow students. (Kerlin 1995, 33)

Taken together, Bobbi Kerlin's work documents the high toll, especially on women, that graduate study too frequently extracts, with lengthened time-to-degree being perhaps the least painful of the consequences:

> of long hours of overwork, of weight loss from stress and anxiety, of weight gain from inactivity, of self-enforced isolation, of disturbed sleep patterns—of experiences that more closely resemble cult-like behaviours than they do the performance of [academic] olympians. (1995, 33)

Could such experiences be what universities intend? Expect? Consider truly necessary to completing the degree? If so, why? In writing from what she calls a "student advocacy" stance, Hawley offers some disturbing conjectures:

> When students' emotional states are considered at all, it is assumed that emotional suffering is not only inevitable, it is actually good for them. I don't know whether this is some form of latent puritanism (if it hurts, it must be good for you) or an indirect way of getting even for one's own travails as a student. I do know that adherents of this philosophy seem to equate caring with coddling. One well-published, dignified old-timer declared that he had gone through bloody hell writing his dissertation and wasn't about to hold any student's hand. "Besides," he added, "a little suffering is good for 'em." (1993, 20–21)

No wonder the word "hazing" arises so often in student reflections on their experience. Given its obvious relationship to fraternity hazing—a process of suffering by which a candidate proves himself "worthy" to join the established company—this perspective seems nothing short of dangerous. As in fraternity hazing, the abuse in graduate study has thrived to an extent that has finally produced not only severe psychological damage, but also a growing number of lifeless bodies.

It is time to challenge the notion that caring about student welfare equates to coddling. As Chapman and Sork suggest, it is time to start questioning the entire enterprise from "different ethical perspectives—of care, of justice and of duty" (1999, 2).

A Critical Perspective on Graduate Education

For those who have eyes to see and ears to hear, there is an abundance of evidence that graduate students commonly suffer severe exploitation and abuse. Like Hawley and the Kerlins, we begin with the assumption that such a situation is unethical and unconscionable. Also like the Kerlins, we insist that the voices of graduate students be heard. However, in this text we intend to move from those assertions into an adjoining area by refocusing a central question: We ask not why so many students leave doctoral programs, but why so many talented adults submit, most often silently, to intolerable conditions, and persevere until completing their degree? With the exception of growing unionization of teaching assistants and a very few personal accounts of particularly outrageous experiences (Cude 1988; Salo 1999), students most commonly do whatever is required of them—however unreasonable or damaging—without protest. But these are smart and articulate people: Why their apparent silent submission?

The answer, of course, is that the institution, its functionaries, and its faculty have power over the students' fate, and with each day in a program, students have more of their investment to lose. It's possible to fail exams even if one knows the material; it can become virtually impossible to have a proposal approved or to get access to an advisor; it's possible to fail a dissertation defense. Even with the most impressive intelligence and commitment, it's entirely possible to spend years of one's time, incalculable amounts of energy, and thousands of dollars only to leave the institution without the desired degree. Students remain silent because speaking out is dangerous—and they know it.

> So that no one thinks I am paranoid, I should say that I have been threatened before (as I will recount) for speaking my mind. I caved. I caved utterly, and while I despise myself for doing it, I don't see what else I could have done. . . . Fear seems to have been the dominant emotion caused by my graduate school experience. (Salo 1999)

Such accounts come only after students have left the institution, which by then has no power over them (as is true for both Cude and Salo). Even when promised anonymity, students are fearful to speak about their experiences. For example, students whose voices are quoted throughout the following pages of this text required extensive assurance that their anonymity would be protected, and one student went so far as to submit her story in writing via U.S. mail, not trusting the confidentiality of her university e-mail account and fearing severe repercussions if she were identified as a source for this text. Another source agreed to an interview over a glass of wine during a collegial social hour, but woke the next morning too frightened to carry out the promise and refused to speak with the researchers at all. Fear among graduate students is a real and rampant phenomenon.

The point that students remain silent because of implicit and explicit threats to their welfare seems an obvious one, but like many obvious "truths" its apparent simplicity is deceptive. An unequal power arrangement is inherent in any "student" position, and power is never simple—most especially when it's embodied in sanctioned, unequal relationships. In addition to creating an additional space for student voices, this text seeks to unravel some of the complexities of power in graduate education so that ethical students, faculty, and administrators alike can better understand (and, we trust, consciously challenge) the dynamics that produce unjust outcomes. The logical starting place for such a project seems to lie naturally in the perspective that critical theory offers. A detailed explanation of a critical perspective is beyond the scope of this text. However, the following sketch of common critical principles and terms may offer readers some useful background as they approach the following chapters.

In the most general terms, critical theory is interested in situations where unequal power arrangements are a clear disadvantage to the less powerful group. In this study, for example, graduate students are obviously a less powerful group whose best interests are often sacrificed to the interests of the dominant faculty/institution group. The critical theorist seeks to uncover the hidden workings of power and help the disadvantaged consciously understand how they are being kept at a disadvantage, and also how their implicit consent has kept them in their subordinate place. The aim of critical theory, then, is to promote more equitable and just power arrangements wherever one group benefits at the expense of another. In the case of this text, it is to promote more equitable and just power arrangements within graduate education. The means to this end involve exposing and questioning the many implicit facets of power that lie hidden in any "normal" state of affairs.

In outlining forms of critical research identified by Fischer, Cherryholmes (1988) precisely captures the heart of the analysis found in the following pages:

> This critical research questions the criteria and standards that previously had been accepted without question. They include: (1) are outcomes equitable and just; (2) do they promote the advantage of all; and, if not, (3) is it possible to alter social practices and institutions to further the advantage of all? (113)

We believe that *all* stakeholders, not just institutions of various kinds, should benefit from graduate education—and that means attending to student experience and outcomes. We also believe that once injustices are uncovered, it will be essential to explore how practices might be changed "to further the advantage of all," not just the privileged already in positions of power.

Such analysis will employ the particular language of critical theory, especially terms that presume an *oppressive* relationship is in place. Freire, whose work is seminal to critical theory, offers this definition of oppression:

> Any situation in which "A" objectively exploits "B" or hinders his pursuit of self-affirmation as a responsible person is one of oppression. (1981, 40)

Since institutional rhetoric openly discusses graduate students in terms of resources, and since so much of the literature makes clear that the enterprise routinely pursues its own goals at student expense (as even the AAU report acknowledges, if as briefly as possible), it is reasonable to talk of graduate students being in an *oppressive* situation.

Moreover, certain characteristics that Freire (1981) identifies as inherent in oppressive situations are also clearly evident in graduate education:

> the oppressed feel like "things" owned by the oppressor. For the latter, *to be* is *to have,* almost always at the expense of those who have nothing. For the oppressed, at a certain point in their existential experience, *to be* is not to resemble the oppressor, but *to be under* him, to depend on him. Accordingly, the oppressed are emotionally dependent. (51)

In graduate education, students are clearly the "things" owned by the university and used to the institution's own advantage. Many common practices reflect this arrangement. For example, limited resources are spread thinly to attract as many students as possible rather than fully funding fewer students. Institutions routinely compete with each other based on how many students they can boast of having in a program, regardless of whether the program can serve those students well or not. Students are often forced to shape dissertations according to prevailing theory in a department rather than their own beliefs. Any number of such practices make clear that those who *have* power and a personal and institutional reputation use graduate students—who are wholly dependent upon the institution and faculty—to serve their own goals. The expense to graduate students be damned—"suffering is good for 'em."

Graduate students are unavoidably dependent: usually financially, always practically, and so unavoidably emotionally. A predictable result is one already noted as characteristic of graduate students:

> The dependent society is by definition a silent society. Its voice is not an authentic voice, but merely an echo of the voice of the [more powerful]. (Freire 1985, 73)

Like other oppressed groups, graduate students do not voice their own perceptions of graduate school as they experience it; instead, they learn very quickly what it is dangerous to say and how necessary it is to echo the voices and values of their supervisors, on topics ranging from theoretical stance in a field, to the appropriate feelings for a researcher to have about child bearing.

Also, readers will benefit from keeping in mind an overview of the critical theorist's perspective on how oppressive relationships are cultivated and maintained. The critical theorist speaks often of the *hegemony* inherent in oppressive relationships—meaning that the dominant group maintains its power without overt action because the subordinate group is conditioned by the culture at large to accept their less powerful place in the status quo without question. In other words, existing relationships are somehow sanctioned by the culture simply as *the way things are.* Many wives, for example, having been saturated with media images of "good wives and mothers" and having been nurtured by a particular kind of mother themselves, have accepted, without question, that their place is in the home and their implicit responsibility is to make other members of their family happy, at any expense to themselves. That's just what mothers and wives *do*—or so many women believed until very recently. Critical theorists refer to the mindset that unconsciously adopts and endorses such exploitive relationships as *constructed consciousness,* a mental framework absorbed from the surrounding culture.

Another common term is *reification,* which applies when some dated practice is unquestioningly continued in a culture. For example, many schools began the practice of suspending lessons in summer because children were needed at home to help with the summer harvest. Although the agrarian way of life has long since passed for most families, summer vacation from school remains a reified—that is, largely unchallenged—practice.

Finally, the word *capital* is used to describe a variety of resources that can help buy entry into the dominant group. *Cultural capital,* for example, refers to certain personal characteristics that are necessary in order to be accepted into the top levels of a hierarchy: certain forms of language, familiarity with certain kinds of art, comfort with certain forms of eating rituals (e.g., knowing the difference between a dinner fork and a salad fork). In this work, *institutional capital* refers generally to anything the institution uses to buy its way into top rankings, including numbers of graduate students and the number of publications produced by its faculty. Again, as in the AAU report, graduate students are cast as *institutional capital* when institutional rhetoric focuses on them as *assets* to the university in ways that ignore or negate the students' humanity.

Through this very particular lens of critical theory, and by employing its particular language and methodology, the following pages examine a variety of elements in the graduate enterprise. This book sheds light on how power relationships affect lived experiences in graduate schools, and how things could be otherwise.

CHAPTER 2

Sources of Institutional Power
Constructed Consciousness, Hegemony, and Reification

> *We may be tempted to ignore [criticism] on the grounds that the professoriate always knows best and that we, as priests of the temple, are the sole guardians and dispensers of knowledge. We should contemplate long-lost religions and civilizations who doubtless held the same views.*
> —DAVID TRIGGLE, UNIVERSITY OF BUFFALO

For years, in private conversations and extensive lore, graduate students have complained about faculty neglect, about exploitation, about success and failure depending more on whim and politics than on ability and work—about widespread institutional and faculty abuse. Yet they continue to enroll, and for the most part endure without public complaint, paying thousands of dollars for the privilege of suffering. It is only recently that a very few, very angry students have become fully open about their experiences (Cude 1988; Salo 1999) and that public evidence of student resistance on a larger scale has appeared (Leatherman 1996, 1998; AAUP Committee on Graduate Students). Still, despite some recent drop in enrollment (AAU 1999) and some notable attrition (Anderson 1998, 1) thousands of graduate students stay and endure whatever oppressive conditions they encounter in their programs. Why?

Part of the answer, of course, is that students anticipate increased earning power and/or want to enter a field otherwise closed to them. But we suggest that other factors also come into play. Specifically, we analyze how common experiences nurture a particular constructed consciousness among prospective graduate students—one that presumes institutional hegemony, discourages questioning of the institution, and ultimately helps sustain reified practice.

CONSTRUCTED CONSCIOUSNESS: LESSONS FROM EXPERIENCE

Consider this student's experience.

> I can still remember the day my admission letter came in the mail. I sat, staring at the envelope, afraid to open it, afraid to see the school's judgment of me. If it was an acceptance, then finally I would be judged certifiably smart—and the honors I'd earned in six years and two degrees would suddenly seem valid—even though they came from a no-name local college. If I got into an Ivy League grad school, then I had to be smart. Right? And the other alternative was impossibly terrifying. I sat there holding that letter a long, long time before I opened it. (H.)

What factors contributed to this student's terror? Why did she feel this way?

Lessons from Past Schooling

Perhaps nothing is so pervasive about education as number and rank: grades 1–12, with the easiest first, or on the bottom, and the most difficult last, or at the top of the grade level ladder. From the earliest days, the goal of every spelling and math test is to earn the greatest possible number of points. At the top of the peak, graduation, the student with the highest grade point average is singularly honored as class valedictorian, the reward for climbing perhaps .01 percent beyond the average of the second best student. In between are standardized tests with the objective being to place in the top percentile, above all the students grouped in the remaining 90 percent—themselves placed into percentiles and quartiles. The hierarchy is evident in the most common terms used to describe elements of the entire process: *highest* grades, *lowest* scores, *top* percentiles, *bottom* quartiles, *above* average, *below* a certain GPA.

By the time students graduate from high school they've long since accepted numbers as reliable indicators in all kinds of evaluations. They take special courses hoping to raise their SAT and ACT scores, and they scramble in their junior and senior years to increase their high school GPAs. They examine statistics to help identify colleges they'll apply to — percentage of tenured faculty and full professors (higher is better), average class size (lower is better), numbers of volumes in the library, numbers of acres on campus, number of graduates employed within a year after graduation, number of sports facilities and clubs, the percentage of students who enroll in graduate study. Every conceivable element of the educational enterprise is counted, reported, and ranked. From the moment a five-year old sets foot in a kindergarten classroom until she leaves formal education, she is on a ladder reaching ever upward toward some academic Olympian height.

Moreover, several times in the process, moving forward means dropping from the pinnacle of one phase to the depths of the next one: this year's kindergarten student graduates to first grade—the lowest of the numerically ranked twelve; this year's cocky eighth grader is next year's gullible high school freshman who can't open his locker; this year's high school senior is next year's wet-behind-the-ears first year college student who can't find her classrooms. Over and over, students in all kinds of educational institutions climb upward to some pinnacle only to drop back to the bottom again when they move on to some newly achieved level. They learn to expect it, and to accept a lowly position when they move *up* from one level to another. They learn to expect the arrogance of the more erudite teachers and the scorn of the more experienced students on higher rungs of the new ladder. Moreover, while the age gap between student and teacher normally narrows at every plateau, the status of teacher never lessens: all students are outranked not only by other students with more advanced standing, but also by the all-powerful teacher, and later professor, who determines student fate and whose policies, actions, and decisions the wise student avoids questioning at any level.

Based on at least sixteen years of such experience, new graduate students know exactly where they will fit into the institutional hierarchy when they enter a program. Masters students know they rank below doctoral students, and doctoral students are acutely aware of their distance from the busy, often famous and powerful professors at the top. Before they even apply, prospective graduate students know that admission to graduate school will involve again attaining some pinnacle—like graduating *summa cum laude* or with some presidential award—and tumbling to the foot of education's Mount Olympus. The new hierarchy, which establishes the entering student as a relatively powerless supplicant before the professorial gods, is established without question or challenge, as Airaksinen says often happens in hegemonic relationships (1992):

> The field of power is a hidden one. Efficient threats are rarely explicated. The subordinate persons have learned to anticipate them. (108)

New graduate students hardly need lessons in hierarchy: no matter what academic triumph they achieved earlier, their extensive experience in schooling has prepared them to assume a place as the least important and least powerful members of their new homes.

Lessons from Rankings and Institutional Materials

In a consumer-oriented society, those shopping for a graduate school are no less susceptible to any product's claim to be Number One than those shopping for rental cars or antacids. Like savvy shoppers who check *Consumer Reports* before purchasing a car or computer, prospective students pore over rankings of graduate programs available from a wide variety of sources. Of course they want the best possible product for the thousands of dollars their graduate education will cost. And, since no graduate school can exist without students, and if many students consider rankings when applying, then every institution must strive to be ranked as highly as possible. A good bit of institutional energy, then, is devoted to enhancing factors that influence rank. To understand institutional actions and priorities it is necessary to be familiar with which factors earn institutions high places in respected rankings. A look at two of the best known rating systems is instructive.

Both *U.S. News and World Report,* which produces one of the most widely distributed and highly regarded rankings of graduate schools annually, and the National Research Council (NRC), which has now produced two widely distributed reports, include *reputation* as one of two categories of data they collect and analyze. Literature from *U.S. News* notes that

> Experts have long considered reputation a valid measure of academic quality in higher education, and we believe a diploma from an institution known for excellence offers graduates a powerful edge in the competition for good jobs. (Graham & Morse 1999, 2)

In fact, for programs in the arts, sciences, social sciences, library science, and the allied health fields, *U.S. News* actually bases its ranking solely on institutional reputation. Similarly, the NRC Executive Summary (1996) lists "reputational measures" as one of its "two primary types of data" (2).

How exactly is reputation measured? A common procedure is to simply ask those involved in higher education to offer their perceptions. Both the NRC and *U.S. News* solicit the input of faculty; *U.S. News* goes

Sources of Institutional Power

a bit farther both within the academy, by including deans, and outside it, by turning to potential employers like school superintendents, judges and practicing engineers (Graham & Morse 1999, 3).

In addition to surveying various groups for their perceptions of institutional quality, both ranking systems include a second category of purportedly more objective—that is, statistical—measures. Among the counts deemed important in the NRC report are the "number of faculty and number of graduates." Although the report concedes that "a strong positive correlation between the number of faculty and its reputational standing has... not been explored thoroughly," the report also concludes that "By and large, however, top-rated programs in most fields tended to have a larger number of faculty and more graduate students than lower-rated programs" (3). Apparently, the NRC believes that bigger is probably better. A similar attitude applies to other elements, including federal grant support, publication and citation records, and "awards and honors" (4).

The *U.S. News* report, on the other hand, uses language suggesting it is more concerned with quality than with quantity. One factor here is the quality that students bring to an institution, determined by—what else?—students' previous statistical rank:

> The caliber of student that a program attracts—which influences the academic climate—is measured by the average undergraduate grade point average and standardized test scores of the entering class. (Graham & Morse, 2)

Another qualitative concern is "how successfully the program prepared students for success," which is calculated using such factors as median starting pay and other types of compensation (bonuses and so on), and the amount of money spent "per student on faculty salaries, libraries and student support services" (2). Money is simply assumed to be a reliable indicator of institutional quality. The number of dollars and cents spent by the institution and earned by graduates is, then, another element institutions need to increase if they want a desirable rank. Of course, to spend more, institutions need to make more, a fact that may well lead to increased tuition—which is fine, since high tuition also generally enhances an institution's reputation.

Those who do rankings also consider the star quality of an institution's students and faculty and here again former grade point averages, SATs and the reputation of the previous school are considered. Therefore, institutions must also work hard to attract top candidates—largely by bragging about the trophies they've already landed. For example, In "Bringing the Best," an article featuring current fellows and prominently linked to its graduate school home page, Penn State brags about the students it has attracted and openly notes the competition for the highest ranked undergraduates:

> The presence on campus of these young stars—the world's future leaders in academia, government, business, and industry—enriches the University in many ways. It shouldn't be surprising that competition for the very best graduate students, while not as widely followed as the angling for blue-chip athletes, is fierce. (Pacchioli 1998)

The very term *blue-chip* makes clear that top graduate students are openly considered a form of academic currency.

Indeed, in this environment, not only students but also faculty become a sort of institutional capital, whose function becomes to enhance institutional reputation. Stanford's list of its current "community of scholars," for example, sounds more like a description of the institution's holdings in a stock portfolio than a profile of professional staff: 16 Nobel laureates, 3 Pulitzer Prize winners, 1 winner of the Congressional Medal of Honor, 20 MacArthur Fellows, 20 recipients of the National Medal of Science, 3 National Medal of Technology recipients, 204 members of the American Academy of Arts and Sciences, 114 members of the National Academy of Sciences, 72 National Academy of Engineering members, 25 members of the National Academy of Education, 40 American Philosophical Society members, and 6 Wolf Foundation Prize for Mathematics winners.

Schools who attain high rankings feature them prominently to lure the very best students to apply. Stanford, for example, boasts on its graduate study Web site that

> Stanford's excellences across a wide spectrum of graduate studies were reflected in the 1996 National Research Council Report, the nation's most extensive study of Ph.D. programs. In peer rankings published by the Council once per decade, Stanford had 32 programs ranked in the top 10 by academic category.

The promotional literature further stresses the financial support it expends on its students:

In 1997, the Stanford Graduate Fellowship Program was created to ensure funding for outstanding graduate students. More than 230 graduate students began fellowships in 32 fields in 1997 and 1998.

It is understood that readers are to accept NRC rank and a count of fellowships as obvious indicators of quality.

Other schools, fully understanding the value of reputation, link their names with those widely known to be consistently in the top rank. Carnegie Mellon's graduate Web page, for example, notes that its

> graduate schools are thought of as being among the elite programs in the country. For example, in its 1996 rankings of "America's Best Graduate Schools," U.S. News & World Report [sic] magazine ranked Carnegie Mellon's School of Computer Science the best in the nation along with programs at the Massachusetts Institute of Technology, Stanford University and the University of California at Berkeley. (1)

Such hyperbole is not restricted to those in the top tiers, however; it permeates the rhetoric of promotional materials from virtually any institution. For example, one state related, public university, the State University of New York at Buffalo, far outside the lofty realm of Stanford and its ivied counterparts, contains an abundance of phrases typical of institutional Web sites at every level: "outstanding record of research, scholarship, and creative activity . . . world-class . . . ranked among the top ten in their fields . . . forefront . . . ranks among the top twenty-five institutions in the United States." The University of Alabama at Birmingham uses similar rhetoric in its self-description: "a nationally and internationally respected center for educational, research and service programs . . . more than $260 million in active grants and contracts . . . among the top institutions in the country in this respect."

As if such hyperbole, dollar counts, and head counts weren't enough to persuade potential applicants of the incredibly elevated position of any institution—known generally as an *ivory tower*—there is plenty of graphic imagery to remind students of their place in this elevated pecking order. The image that most often confronts viewers on the first screen of Web pages and the front page of promotional materials is a photo of the most impressive physical structure on a campus. Even more importantly, however, the image is most often presented at an angle that positions the viewer at some low level looking *up* at it. And, the top of the image usually involves some tower or other peak, pointing to heaven like a church spire and functioning as a physical symbol of what the entire enterprise is about: reaching some enormously distant and vaguely sacred height.

Inspecting materials specifically designed to impress readers with the elevated status of the institution, the would-be applicant is inundated with numbers and rankings and multiple images of heavenly spires and ivied walls. Does he or she dare approach a top tier school? Is that too high an aspiration? After all, the graduate school Mount Olympus is like any other heaven—no one can be sure of getting in until the judgment is made at the gate. Not everyone who knocks will be permitted to enter.

Lessons from Commercial Materials

In very short order, the challenge of getting in to a desirable school appears formidable to students exploring the possibility. Knowing they are approaching a strange new world, applicants often look for help in learning the ropes and maximizing the chances that their applications will be successful. As they have in the past, when confronting trouble in first year algebra or being faced with SATs or having to choose an undergraduate college, many applicants turn to commercial publishers for special courses and for advice, knowing that they can very probably scan bookshelves or Web sites and find what they seek. Publishers, of course, are ready to meet the demand for any advice in any format a student customer might choose.

In addition to its plethora of books with every conceivable kind of advice for K–12 through college applicants, the Kaplan Web site, for example, offers several publications that both capitalize on and reinforce the perception that potential graduate students should worry a great deal about whether or not they will be judged worthy of admission. Its book page promises that readers can "get the scoop on grad school" from *Kaplan and Newsweek's Careers 2000;* they can get "expert advice [that will help them] get into the graduate school [of choice]" from *Kaplan Newsweek Graduate School Admissions Advisor, 1999;* they can "maximize [their] performance on all sections of the GRE with strategies from the world leader in test preparation" by using *Kaplan GRE 1999–2000—* "a higher score ... guaranteed" ; and, they can "seize the competitive edge in the search for fellowships and grants" with the "incisive" *Yale Daily News Guide to Fellowships & Grants 1999* (Mohamadi 1998). In this last example, as well as several other Kaplan/Yale publications, the name of a top-ranked school is used to impress the aspiring graduate student with the quality and value of the product, again exploiting the power of reputation to compete for the student dollar.

Like Kaplan's, Peterson's Web site contains a wide variety of guides to "help [readers] throughout the various phases of [their] education, career, and life"—a one-stop, advice-on-everything-conceivable site. Various publications are linked to its graduate page, *Graduate Schools in the U.S. 1999*, *Peterson's Compact Guide: Graduate Studies in Education 1999*, and the "bestseller" *How to Write a Winning Personal Statement for Graduate and Professional School, 3rd edition (Stelzer 1997)*—offering information on such topics as: "applying, testing, getting in"; "guidance on how to apply to, fund, and succeed in grad school"; and "expert guidance on choosing an engaging topic, writing clearly, and organizing for impact." Featured, too, are several articles reminding prospective students how precarious their situation is, reinforcing the need for advice and the expectation that success is uncertain: "Questions to Ask Before Hitting the Rough Road to Grad School" (Thomas 1998), for example, or "Transition Issues for Minority Grad Students" (Thomas 1999). Interestingly, such feature articles available on the site often contain links to Peterson's *The Ultimate Grad School Survival Guide* (Mitchell 1996). Even as the articles focus on difficulties, they link to a full text promising to see the student through the entire process, from "getting in" to "the thesis/dissertation."

When would-be applicants delve into this text (and others like it), what kind of language do they encounter? What messages do they receive about undertaking graduate education in books that provide guides to "survival"? A look at Mitchell's *Ultimate Guide* suggests that commercial publishers help reify the formidable reputation of the oh-so-tough-to-get-into-and-survive graduate schools. Even as they purport to help, commercial materials reinforce the idea that aspiring graduate students have no particular reason to expect success. On the contrary, readers are warned that they need to prepare assiduously even to submit a successful application, and then there is a good bit they need to know if they are to "survive."

Consider, for example, Mitchell's response to a subhead in the first few pages of the book asking "What Are the Odds?":

> Many schools are downsizing and restructuring their programs to cut expenses.... In some cases universities have actually reduced the number of students admitted to graduate programs. This reduction is a responsible move by universities reacting to the current academic job

> market and decreased government funding. But it means an even smaller pool of admitted applicants. I know of one student who received his B.A. from a top 10 school, had an "A" average overall GPA, and great GRE scores. He applied to the top 10 universities for graduate school. Not one school accepted him for admission despite his outstanding credentials. His situation may not be the norm, but you should be aware of the competition. Even second-tier schools that used to have less rigorous standards have become extremely competitive, and many of these schools are admitting students from the top 10 universities. It's definitely a buyer's market! (1996, 8–9)

How interesting the rhetoric is here. First, it seems that the prospective student should be grateful to the university for acting in a responsible manner as it whittles down his or her chances of admission to grad school and creates a climate of cut-throat competition. Furthermore, one would think that the student who will be paying thousands of dollars in tuition would be the buyer. But here the institution is the buyer and a finicky one at that. It can pick and choose among its applicants, discarding even qualified students like substandard merchandise.

Apparently, for the student, the odds of getting accepted are poor indeed. It's not surprising that the word *luck* often starts linking itself to the student's thoughts about admission: *If I get into a good school, I'll be one lucky person! After all, so many people don't make it.*

Of course, in Mitchell's book readers get to this information only if they continued reading past page three, where they learn about exams at or near the end of coursework:

> Students dread these—common euphemisms include "The Test From Hell," "The Inquisition," and "The Bloodbath"—and with good reason. Some schools use these tests to weed out less promising students, and study time can take anywhere from three months to two years.

The fainthearted need not apply.

Of course, if admission and survival were easier, people wouldn't need advice from commercial publishers and institutions couldn't enhance their reputations through elitism and . . . so it goes, goes, goes, goes, goes. The fact is that both institutions and commercial enterprises benefit when students perceive first admission and then survival as integral, formidable challenges, and so both institutions and commercial enterprises reinforce those perceptions at every opportunity.

There seems to be an inverse proportion between the prestige of the

Sources of Institutional Power

institution and the power of the student. The institution is presented to the student through rankings and its own promotional materials in terms of superlatives: highest scores; most faculty; largest amounts of money spent on facilities, programs, faculty salaries; smallest classes, acceptance rates, etc. At the same time, students are bombarded with hints about their helplessness: how hard it will be to get into school; how prestigious the school is and how imposing it looks; how smart the other students will be; how much help they will need with taking entrances tests or even writing letters of application. It's a wonder the student has enough confidence to walk to the mailbox.

INSTITUTIONAL HEGEMONY: GRADUATE STUDENT PERCEPTION OF PLACE AND POWER

The Bottom Rung: Student Perception of Place

When application forms are dropped into the mail, how do students understand the position they are in relative to the institution they hope to enter? Consider various elements as a whole:

- By virtue of prior educational experience, graduate applicants expect to assume the lowest position on a new academic ladder.
- Applicants have likely selected the highest ranked programs that they think might accept them—maximizing the distance between their lowly position and the top rung on the ladder they hope to cling to. That is, the higher students aim in the institutional hierarchy, the longer the upward climb they face.
- Prospective grad students have been inundated with rhetoric about the extraordinary intelligence and talent of the experienced students and the faculty at the new institution.
- Graduate applicants have been saturated with messages that it will be difficult to get in, that past excellence is no guarantee they'll be considered good enough to join this new community.
- Applicants have been warned that even if they get in, the road will be arduous—even tortuous—and survival uncertain. Perhaps, even if they gain admission, time will prove that they aren't good enough after all.

Little wonder that students are exhilarated when accepted to a program and enter determined to do whatever it takes to survive what they perceive as the ultimate test of their talent. Becoming affiliated with an institution means being admitted to the presence of the great, and the new student is most often honored and awed by being permitted to join the company. They enter feeling lucky to have been given a chance to prove themselves worthy—and also often in terror that the opposite will result. In essence, students have managed to grasp the bottom rung of a very, very long ladder.

References in personal communications (1999) from students reflect that self-doubt is common. One student commented:

> I have always questioned whether I was good enough for graduate school . . . I always felt less intelligent than the others in my program, and often also felt that I had been admitted by secretarial error. (D.)

D. seems to have bought into the institutional rhetoric about the slim chances of getting into grad school. Sadly, she suspects that her admission to the university was a fluke, an accident, and that she is in some way a fake. Even in retrospect D. doubts her abilities. In another instance, a student with considerable life experience is also surprised by his acceptance into grad school even though he has twice before been in graduate school and garnered good grades.

> I was shocked to be accepted—shocked in a positive way! . . . They only selected about 30% [and] coupled with what I perceived as a poor GRE, I felt that the younger ones would win . . . despite decent grades with the two masters. (G.)

Good grades and previous degrees are not enough, in this student's mind, to offset his age and disadvantageous test scores. Both of these students have made harsh judgments of themselves based on the implicit values of their universities.

Other researchers report similar accounts of student experience, even among the most talented who enter. In a recent edited text (Anderson 1998, 17), Steven Weiland reports that

> John Huchra . . . cosmologist, uncertain of his prospects when he entered the California Institute of Technology in 1970, . . . found himself "intimidated from the word go." Despite his qualifications and high grades he "figured [he] was a dummy" and not as good as the others in his classes. (Lightman & Brawer 1990, 381–382)

Convinced that luck may well have had something to do with admission, with lingering doubts about their own abilities and about their ultimate survival, new graduate students enter the institution with little inclination to question existing power structures and practices. One reason that institutions have so much power over students, then, is simply that students frequently enter assuming that they are taking a "natural" position at the bottom of a new hierarchy, and—like other oppressed groups—accept their apparently powerless position without question, as some sort of natural "way things are."

One of the most obvious sources of institutional power, then, is the constructed consciousness of entering students.

The Invisible Threat: Situated Power and Student Consciousness

The nature of situated power. It may be hard for some to imagine the graduate school experience as an instance of oppression, since many students can—and do—choose to leave when their stress or unhappiness grows too great. Literally, of course, this is true. But applying a more theoretical lens to the situation uncovers a great deal more complexity in exactly how students are enmeshed in power relationships and why they so often quietly endure oppressive practices rather than leave or challenge the accepted practice. Specifically, Wartenberg's conception of "situated power" illuminates the many facets of power that encourage and help maintain student compliance (1992).

In discussing power relationships, many theorists assume a dyadic structure: a powerful agent in place over a subordinate agent. Wartenberg argues, however, that "the power dyad is itself situated in the context of other social relations through which it is actually constituted as a power relationship" (1992, 80). That is, in the most simplistic terms: while power relationships do include one agent with obvious power over another—the teacher who grades student performance, for example—the dominant agent has such power because of elements in the surrounding social context:

> the grade itself, being by nature a sign, does not have an adverse effect on the well-being of the student.... A student's well-being is affected by the grade only through the mediation of human beings situated outside the classroom who use the grade as a sign that results in their administering harm to the student, e.g., by denying him access to the opportunity to further his education. (83–84)

If conferring grades constitutes power, that is true only because someone outside the school (parents, employers or colleges, for example) use grades to make decisions about the student's future. A powerful force in the relationship, then, becomes these "others" who designate some elements of structural relationships (grades assigned to students, recommendations written by professors, GPA's) as significant.

The power that institutions have over students, then, is conferred by a third party, by some agent that specifies that if a student desires X, he or she must submit to an institution's program and earn degree Y. Students, therefore, aware of the importance of letters of recommendation and high GPA's in the world outside of academe are willing, for the most part, to sacrifice their egos and independence at the altar of higher education to attain the rewards offered by the outside agency.

The disempowered student. What are the implications for power relationships in graduate schools? First, it is worth noting that students rarely enter graduate school for the sake of being in graduate school, as is witnessed by increasing criticism of graduate schools for producing Ph.D.'s and others who can't find jobs (AAU 1999). Instead, students perceive graduate study as a necessary means to some desirable end: becoming a university professor, or lawyer, or high-level researcher. When the social agency or field decrees that practitioners in a field need a graduate degree, the student who wishes to work in that field is forced to go to graduate school and complete the requirements of the degree-granting institution. The behavior of graduate students, then, is primarily driven by agents outside the academy—employers or certifying agencies—who require certain degrees and prefer that they be from some institutions rather than others. This sheds additional light on why graduate students are reluctant to leave or to criticize their institutions once they've begun a program:

> The subordinate agent faces a situated power relationship as a given over which he can have little effect but which will have a significant effect upon him. He encounters such situations much as he does natural necessities, as things to which he must submit in order to realize his own desires and intentions. (Wartenburg 86)

Having gained admission through a perilous process, having been warned of the very real possibility of failure, the student is aware that not completing the program would have major impact on his or her career and life goals. In such an environment, the logical behavior is to "submit," to do whatever the institution says needs to be done on whatever timetable and in whatever fashion it specifies. With significant insecurity from the first moment of approach, and with consequences of failure affecting literally the rest of their lives, it is no wonder that students rarely perceive themselves in a position to resist oppression or to imagine productive rebellion. Instead, they comply:

> the subordinate agent comes to adopt certain courses of action for the instrumental purpose they have in allowing him to realize his purposes. But this process is precisely one of subjection, i.e., the creation of the human agent as having desires that are adopted by the human being as his own due to his interaction with a power structure over which he has no control. (Wartenburg 100)

Students may believe they want to attend the highest possible ranked school, to earn A's, to write an award-winning dissertation, to complete a doctorate, but such goals are strictly instrumental and formed outside the students. The social agents in the background—employers and such—actually empower the institutions by valuing certain kinds of degrees from certain kinds of institutions. Graduate students, then, willingly submit to the institution and adopt its values because of their long-term goals in relation to the social agents. Though they may frequently suffer, they are loathe to question openly existing power arrangements in the community. Their situation is as Freire says of all oppressed groups (1985):

> The dependent society introjects the values and life style of the metropolitan [i.e., dominant] society, since the structure of the latter shapes that of the former.... The dependent society is by definition a silent society. (73)

Students, then, don't challenge the institution because they are part of it and are so positioned that they have too much to lose. The social agents outside the institution which nevertheless account for its situated power generally trust the universities to do a good job and rarely (if ever) inquire closely into educational practices. Who, then, asks of university practices "Why?" and "With what effects?" Who zealously monitors ethical behavior and humane treatment? No one. And the results are as predictable as they are dismal.

REIFICATION: INSTITUTIONS THAT CAN DO NO WRONG

After formally applying to a graduate school where I'd taken several courses, I received as reply a letter asking for my GRE scores. I dutifully forwarded my copy (both raw and percentile scores, in their original postmarked envelope, with the original accompanying correspondence) to the grad school GCR (gargoyle in charge of records).

"Sorry," he said. "I need an official copy of your scores and besides that, your scores are too old; you need to retake the GRE or some other test."

I refused. My scores were excellent; my grades in the courses I had taken, high; and my disposable time, limited. The Chair of the Department didn't see a need for me to retest, nor did my advisor, nor did my instructor. Nobody did, in fact, except for the registrar. I consulted him again. He was adamant.

"Your scores are too old."

"I'm the same person who took the exam, and every one else at the university is willing to accept these scores."

"You must take the Graduate Record Exam again."

"No, I have already taken it and scored in the 96th percentile in my field."

"OK, then, take the GRE's again and we'll accept the higher scores."

"Then why not just accept these scores now as high enough?"

"Because you have to take the GRE's." (K.)

Such incidents, evocative of the well-known "Who's on first?" comedy routine, are just as circular and not nearly as funny as the Abbott and Costello dead-end exchange. Though "survivors" often tell such stories later in life to entertain others, for students who have often put their personal lives on hold for several years and who have invested thousands of dollars (which they usually don't have and can't afford), there is nothing funny about living through such frustrations. Especially since they are common. The community of graduate students is flooded with tales of student time, energy, money and sanity being squandered because an institution refused to examine or change a rule or a ruling.

Indeed, the woman quoted above was again thwarted by similar idiocy after receiving an Ivy League doctorate when she tried to enroll in a graduate course elsewhere. Asked to submit her undergraduate transcripts, she noted that she held a doctorate in the same field and that she didn't want to enroll in a program but simply to take a course she found interesting. To no avail: no undergraduate transcripts, she was told, no course.

Infuriated, she went home and retrieved her actual doctoral diploma, complete with institutional seal and again, the original envelope. This time the results were slightly better: the functionary agreed to call "upstairs" to see if the diploma could be accepted in lieu of the undergraduate transcript to allow the good doctor to enroll in a course. "Well," she heard the functionary say *sotto voce* into the receiver, "it *looks* real. There's a lot of gold and the letters feel sort of bumpy."

Such are the absurd results when no one can or will challenge institutional senility: the institution clings to habits that have long since stopped serving any useful purpose—like an old woman in a nursing home who continues ironing motions with empty hands and wasted arms—and the senselessness goes on and on. If most students continue to comply with requirements simply because they *are* requirements, then the institution has no particular reason to examine a system that seems to be working. And if the social agents that empower the institution care only about degrees awarded and not about the requirements en route, why *would* the institution change? Here, an adaptation of an old adage applies: "If it ain't broke *for us,* don't even think about fixing it." Certainly if "it" isn't broke for those in power, nothing will be done. They are anxious to maintain the structures in place. And if students are unhappy or inconvenienced? That would be their problem. And the problem would remain a problem.

This might be a less important point if instances of such inanity were most often frustrating but still relatively minor, as in paying for still more paperwork or taking yet another exam. But that is not the case. To understand how high the cost of institutional intractability can be for the student involved, consider this long, sad tale posted on a Web site by a student who enrolled in a summer course to meet a university requirement:

> The major problem was that I had unwittingly broken the university rules for maintaining my Javits fellowship. According to these rules, summer courses must be taken during the General Summer Session to count toward fellowship maintenance. My course took place too early in the summer. It didn't count. At all.

> Mind you, there was nothing wrong with the course itself or my progress in it. It counted for graduate credit, and it carried enough credits to satisfy all the other rules. It simply took place during the wrong summer session. . . .
>
> I had . . . two options. I could lose the fellowship (with no time left to find other funding). Or I could retroactively register for research credits during the correct summer session, take an Incomplete, and work off the Incomplete during the fall. I had a very busy fall, but I essentially had no choice but to take on the research credits, if I cared to eat during the next year.

Unlike most students, this one actually took the step of trying to call attention to the apparent silliness of the rule:

> I wrote a very stiff letter to [the university functionary involved], to the dean who supervised her, and to the Javits Fellowship supervisor at the U.S. Department of Education . . . [asking not for a reversal in my case, but for a general] change in the rule. I received no response from the dean. I got an email from [the university functionary] . . . saying nothing could be done for me. . . . The Department of Education official apparently called the university and was assured the situation was being handled. He sent me an email to that effect.
>
> But the rule has not been changed. (Salo 1999)

Forced to take on more work than she could reasonably handle in the fall semester, Salo eventually vented—under a pseudonym—on an Internet bulletin board, where the functionary's daughter happened to read the tale and identify the players, pseudonym or not. She was subsequently also pressured into removing her notes from the bulletin board, apologizing in writing to functionary and dean both, as well as agreeing to stop talking about the incident (under threat of academic harm). The ultimate outcome provoked far more than frustration and extra work:

> This contretemps scared me badly and shook my belief in the university. I spent a couple of weeks not sleeping and not eating decently. I was very close to leaving. I decided that I was going to forego my final year of Javits eligibility, just to get out from under the heel of the Fellowships Office. . . . It is difficult to measure the economic consequence of this decision, because there are

> several different ways to think about its monetary value, but for what it's worth: the yearly stipend was $14,400 and the fellowship paid all my tuition.

Of course, this is Salo's version of what happened, and there are two sides to every story. Hers, however, is openly posted on the Internet with all the documentation she can provide and with invitations to others to contribute contrasting views. She posted her story, however, only *after* she chose to leave the university, which subsequently lost its power to silence her.

Here, we pause to reiterate that this entire book—as Salo says of her work—details specific anecdotes not to vilify particular people and institutions, but instead to provide exemplars of common *systemic* problems. Individual oppressive actions are enabled by an oppressive culture. If the *culture* of an institution is hierarchical and rigid, then its members are apt to endorse and exploit the privileges of hegemony and to become increasingly rigid themselves . . . very likely resulting in mindless enforcement of existing policies and resistance to change. The culture permits abuse, and so encourages it; people who may believe they're using their power for the "greater good" of the institution increasingly resist any challenge to the status quo.

This is, in fact, the sort of behavior that David Triggle (1997), Dean of the Graduate School of SUNY Buffalo, describes as common among faculty at his institution—and we believe it would be the rare dean in any institution who didn't endorse the following as an all-too-accurate description:

> Recent public and printed utterances from among our faculty argue that contemplation of change is either premature, unnecessary or both [and certainly inconvenient]; that any change will destroy the university overnight; that change will foster destructive competition; that all resources should be left in the originating departments; that faculty are being told what they ought to be researching; that we will end up as a market economy, that our fundamental disciplines [as opposed to "those professional ones"] are being marginalized; and that we are turning ourselves into a "teaching institution" or worse. We are apparently on our way to Hell in a hand-basket!! (1)

Institutional policies and institutional members alike are rigid, often absurdly so in the face of reasonable criticism, largely because there is no reason for them to be otherwise. Structural hierarchy means that those on the top of any particular heap need not answer to anyone below. Registrars have ultimate power over enrollment and other administrative details once policies are set, and outside of their own humanity, have little reason to care how powerless students experience those policies. Faculty, of course, by virtue of tenure and rank, can't really be forced to do anything by anyone—as administrators are quick to complain. Of course, administrators have their own set of weapons in the power game: they control the university budget. And as usual, money translates to power.

Contrary to public rhetoric, the "community" said to exist within universities is a myth. The population of every campus is divided into neat sub-hierarchies, and the expected, and approved, behavior at every level is to keep one's gaze directed upward. No need to heed those below: what can *they* do? Little wonder that no one is more acutely aware of this cultural climate than the students at the bottom of the graduate school food chain; little wonder that they so rarely find a voice, and that so few of the powerful ever listen when they do speak.

If we contemplate ancient religions and lost civilizations as David Triggle suggests in the epigraph to this chapter, would we find any parallels to modern graduate institutions? Perhaps. Prepared by their own prior academic experience and the sages of academic and institutional rhetoric, students come as willing acolytes to worship at the temple of graduate education, to submit themselves to the ministrations of faculty priests and to the rites and rituals of academe. Everyone in the system, a constellation of competing groups all with powers directly affecting the graduate experience, knows his or her place and its parameters. Given constructed consciousness, hegemony, and reification, would anyone dare to violate the rules, to step out of place, to disturb the order, to consider alternatives, to examine the rituals, to innovate?

CHAPTER 3
Institutional Cultures and Power
The Minefield of Conflicting Identities

> *Peaceable kingdoms aren't born; they're made. And that is why it seems to me that the university, like other places of employment, needs to become aware of itself as a social organism.*
> —JANE TOMPKINS

THE INFLUENCE OF CULTURE ON BEHAVIOR

To untangle various perspectives and conflicts within higher education, some researchers have found it useful to use *culture* as an organizing principle. Chaffee and Tierney, for example, define the concept and explain why it is a powerful tool for analyzing behavior (1998):

> The most fundamental construct of an organization, as of a society, is its culture. An organization's culture is reflected in what is done, how it is done, and who is involved in doing it. This concerns decisions, actions, and communication both on an instrumental and a symbolic level. (7)

To better understand why people within an organization behave as they do, it is useful to understand the organization's culture, most especially its value and reward systems.

Organizational culture embodies a value system that determines which behaviors will be honored and rewarded. As a result, culture strongly influences behavior within the organization. Because rewards come to those employees whose behavior supports organizational values, most employees shape their behavior to fit the culture's value system. At one institution, for example, faculty might invest most of their energy in innovative and effective teaching because they know good teaching will be rewarded with promotion. At another institution, however, faculty might invest most of their time and energy pursuing multi-million dollar grants because that is the work that will be rewarded with promotion. New faculty must always ask "What's important at this institution?" so that they know how to proceed in pursuit of tenure and promotion.

Besides promotion and pay increases, less tangible rewards are also available. Those who behave in approved ways normally experience increased power—both implicit and explicit. Increased rank, for example, brings increased privilege, as in freedom to teach whatever one wants, whenever one wants. Or, if the media pays attention to a research project, then the researcher is rewarded with high visibility within the institution, making its president more likely to be interested in the researcher's stance on a funding issue.

To understand how power plays out in universities, then, it's helpful to identify institutional cultures and their impact on behavior. As Rorty says (1992),

> To understand power, we need to consider the way that structures constrain and direct individuals, the ways that political and economic structures define interactions among individuals and groups. That is why power is often invisible; it is not lodged in any individual person or institution. The structures of institutions determine the flow of authority; the structure of an economy determines access to goods and services; the structure of social arrangements determines the legitimacy of voice. It is through and in these that power is exercised, as enabling or limiting interests and their satisfaction. It is these that construct the mentality that forms a culture's conceptions of its interests. (1992, 10)

To understand a culture, then, is to better understand the choices and the power—or lack of power—that people experience within it.

CULTURE AS AN INTERPRETIVE LENS

As there are several ways to conceive of groups within higher education, there are several ways to conceive of culture within the field. Limiting analysis to a single conception means limiting understanding, for every member of the field belongs to more than one group: the administrator is also male or female, full or part-time, some specific race, and some specific nationality. Because the values of various cultures may be in conflict, the impact of culture on behavior is perhaps best understood by considering multiple cultures in play simultaneously.

This is the approach Austin (1990) has taken in analyzing multiple cultures that faculty members inhabit, an approach that will be extended in this chapter. She posits

> four primary cultures that influence faculty values and behaviors: the academic profession, the discipline, the academy as an organization within a national system, and the specific type of institution. (62)

Essentially, here Austin identifies four co-existing cultures within the academy. The culture she identifies as *the academic profession* is the culture of the professoriate, or the way professors define their role as professional academics—as opposed to the way administrators might define their role, for example. The culture Austin identifies as *the discipline* is the culture of an academic specialty, or the culture shared by academics interested in the same academic subject—the culture of sociologists as opposed to chemists, for example. *Academy as an organization* is Austin's term for the culture that all institutions of higher education share—the culture of all colleges and universities as opposed to K–12 education or trade schools. Finally, *culture of institutional type* is Austin's term for the culture shared by institutions of a similar type—the culture of community colleges, for example, as opposed to the culture of research universities.

While Austin's work focuses on how these cultures affect faculty behavior, the framework she provides has larger possibilities, especially in terms of graduate education. Graduate students are directly affected by the behavior of faculty, staff, and administrators, each of whom acts in ways that will bring them rewards in the particular culture they find primary. A teaching assistant might have trouble getting help from the tenured professor who believes teaching introductory level classes is beneath him or her, as professorial culture often suggests. When all institutions begin pushing their faculty to publish, a graduate student may find his or her department poorly funded and able to offer few courses if it is not producing copious research. In a department where the prevailing disciplinary culture has valued only empiricist research for decades, a graduate student expressing interest in constructivist research may face outright hostility. A graduate student who says that teaching in a community college is his or her career goal will soon be alienated in a prestigious research institution.

It seems evident that each of these cultures affect not only faculty, but also graduate students and perhaps others in the academy as well. In this chapter, we extend Austin's work into a new area, examining the impact of the four cultures she identifies on graduate education. This analysis of values, behaviors and power arrangements in each of the cultures as they affect graduate study exposes a minefield of multiple and complex power arrangements that imperil graduate students.

The Culture of Higher Education

All institutions of higher education share (at least rhetorically) some cultural values of the academy, some characteristics that make them what they are—educational institutions—as opposed to something else, like commercial enterprises. Austin includes among these "the belief that the central goal is good work and that the rewards are the collegiality, the autonomy, and the intellectual discovery and sharing" (65). Few members of the academy would disagree that these values are central to higher education. These assumptions are implicit in such common academic terms as *community of scholars* and *intellectual freedom.* The mission of higher education is, literally, to offer its members something *higher* than daily life: more time to think, to read, to discuss, to innovate, to research, to pursue truth, to somehow promote a better tomorrow. These are, then, the academy's professed values. As Austin argues, however, the professed values are much more rhetorical than they are real.

Cultural change has come to the university over time, as it has to every other element of modern life:

> Cultural shifts threaten . . . to increase the influence of organizational characteristics more typically associated with other sectors of the work force—increased competition at the expense of colleagueship, fewer intrinsic rewards, less normative commitment to the institution, less "lofty" personal and institutional goals. (66)

Here, Austin notes the effect of the competitions outlined in Chapter Two, noting especially losses in collegiality and commitment to the institution. Other critics charge that changes have been even deeper and more damaging to the cultural values that higher education professes to embody. Martin Anderson is damning in his assessment of the current status of traditional values (1996):

> We once thought of universities and colleges as special places, places of teaching and learning, places for the pursuit of truth, but above all, as temples of integrity. Integrity is the soul of intellectual life; it infuses

Institutional Cultures and Power

> thinking and writing with soundness and veracity. . . . "Integrity without knowledge is weak and useless, and knowledge without integrity is dangerous and dreadful." . . . [But it] has been quite a while since anyone spoke of the world of American higher education as a place of integrity. For good reason. . . . The death of integrity in the heart of higher education is the root cause of the educational troubles which afflict us today. (9)

While not all critics would go so far as Anderson, who titles his book *Impostors in the Temple*, certainly many would agree, as we do, that few institutions behave according to the traditional values that they profess in mission statements and public speeches. Students are quick to note such discrepancies between what institutions say and what they *do*. Less gently than Austin, for example, the student conversation below identifies the shift that Anderson describes as a "leap from a secluded retreat of quiet thought to one of America's bustling big businesses" (30):

> *First student:* I keep wondering how we can get ahead if we can't trust our advisors and teachers. They tell you one thing in the classroom, but they act in a different way. You need to get a profile of their personality. It's very unfair because when you come back to school you think it's going to be heaven, that you'll be able to discuss anything. . . . Why do we suffer this injustice? I expected so much of everybody, but you realize it's not so fantastic. I expected much more intellectually—you realize it's not like that.
> *Second student (in response):* Well, it's the corporate model.
> *(Personal communication, October 21, 1998)*

Not the heaven students imagine before they enter, not a place where mentors can be trusted, not a place where it's safe to expose one's thinking, graduate school resembles instead the dog-eat-dog corporate model, whose greatest value is always the bottom line.

Essentially, while institutions may still profess allegiance to the values of a unifying and lofty traditional culture, it is not one that guides their behavior. Early disillusionment for students, who do not yet have reason to doubt the sincerity of the rhetoric, is common:

> I was so excited when I was accepted—I believed that I passed some really really stringent requirements to get into the place.

> After all, it was ranked in the top three nationwide. Imagine how I felt when I later found out that during the time I applied, every applicant was accepted no matter what their credentials were. The department wanted to add another professor and they couldn't do that until they'd increased their enrollment. I thought I was a good candidate for doctoral study, but what I turned out to be was one of many bodies being used as bargaining chips. (D.)

What students need to understand, then, is that of the four cultures Austin identifies, academic culture is *not* the one that drives institutional and personal behavior. Academic culture is the one that drives rhetoric—and only rhetoric. Graduate students who assume that institutions will act in accordance with their rhetoric, or on professed values like integrity and intellectual freedom, are likely to find themselves at least disappointed and possibly cheated or betrayed.

In addition to values, either real or rhetorical, another significant element of the academy's culture is bureaucratic structure, which has a tremendous impact on students. Bureaucracy, however, is most usefully discussed in terms of conflict between bureaucrats and other institutional groups. Examples of such conflicts are so ubiquitous that they appear throughout this text, as in the Chapter Two discussion of student difficulties stemming from a bureaucrat's refusal to reconsider or bend a policy or procedure. Because we feel this point is amply detailed in many other places, we'll offer only a very few examples here and move on.

The following anecdote suggests how easy it is for a bureaucracy to insist that any problem a student has belongs to the student and not to the institution:

> The lab coordinator, who is supposed to set up all labs, was keeping pictures of naked women on his office (university owned) computer. When I complained to him he said he'd been here so long that there was nothing the department or university could do so I should just live with it. When I complained to the department, the department chair passed it on to the assistant chair who showed my letter to the lab coordinator. The assistant chair told me "John is John and there's nothing we can do" and then John stopped speaking to me, and also stopped getting necessary equipment for my students' labs. Also, after that semester ended I was informed by the professors that I could no

longer teach courses because John refused to work with me. They removed me from the list to teach the next semester and hired undergraduates to do it instead. But at least the pictures are gone now. I guess that's something. (J.)

The lesson is clear: students challenge inappropriate, offensive (and possibly illegal) behavior of any entrenched member of the institution at their peril. Faced with a student concern, administrators and others are far more likely to avoid ruffling feathers than to confront an established and powerful bureaucratic dragon.

Bureaucratic abuse surfaces in countless ways every day. A student might be forced to trudge from office to office because one department refuses to help identify another appropriate resource; a student might experience a six-month delay in progress because he or she—or his or her advisor—turned in a particular piece of paper six hours late; a student might be disliked by a department secretary and find it impossible to get a message to or an appointment with his or her advisor. Anyone with any experience with higher education is likely to know all too well that bureaucratic problems are so pervasive that in themselves they constitute a significant obstacle to earning a graduate degree.

The Culture of Specific Institutional Type

While all institutions are thought to share some overarching goals, various kinds of institutions are also assumed to have differentiated missions and resulting differences in value and reward systems. Austin, for example, suggests that major universities are expected to emphasize research; state colleges, research and teaching; liberal arts, teaching and institutional commitment; community colleges, teaching and the intrinsic rewards of working with students (67). Of course, whatever the emphasis of a particular type of institution, its formal mission statement is sure to include the goal of good teaching. Again, however, a discrepancy between professed values and real values is evident:

> One would have to go back to pre-World War Two days to find a university environment in which teaching was valued in equal measure with research, despite lip service to the contrary.... In the 1980s, Clark Kerr, then president of the University of California at Berkeley, observed that the focus upon research had given rise to the veneration of the non-teacher; the higher a professor's standing, the less he

or she has to do with students! This trend has continued almost unabated, particularly at four-year doctorate-granting universities. (Hawley 1993, 24)

Unhappily, the university reverence for research has recently saturated institutions of all kinds. In recent years, many traditional liberal arts colleges have, in fact, sought reclassification as universities and gone into the research and doctorate-granting business. For example, one of the authors of this text (Hinchey) has two examples in her own back yard in northeastern Pennsylvania. Wilkes College, where she earned a bachelor's degree, is now Wilkes University; in the nearby Scranton area, Marywood, formerly a woman's liberal arts college, is now a co-ed university. When two liberal arts colleges seek university status in such a small geographic pond (an area not only historically opposed to change, but also already housing a competing, well-established Jesuit university), a much larger trend seems obvious.

Why the increasing institutional shift toward a research mission and away from a focus on teaching? Austin traces the link between this change and increasing emphasis on status (which, as demonstrated in Chapter 2, breeds recruiting power):

> [T]he research university is the model that all other institutions strive to emulate. The widespread acceptance of this hierarchy has made research 'the central professional endeavor and the focus of academic life' (Rice 1986, 14); it is accepted as the route to national status. (63)

The research university leads the way, then, and many other institutions—despite their original classification and purported specialized mission—have increasingly embraced research as their strongest institutional value.

Many have been critical of the emphasis on research to the detriment of teaching. Chaffee and Tierney's assessment is typical (1998):

> [T]he criteria for campus reward systems increasingly emphasize scholarly productivity as evidenced by the number of publications. Yet, in many colleges and universities, an overemphasis on research as a criteria for reward ignores realities of heavy teaching loads and increasing numbers of students requiring special assistance... [R]esearch specialization, when taken to an extreme, can obscure the fact that good teaching requires more than excellence in research. (68)

Institutional Cultures and Power

Many researchers and writers reiterate the criticism that teaching suffers as institutional rewards are increasingly tied to research productivity. Good teaching does not ensure tenure, nor does poor teaching lead inevitably to tenure denial:

> Even in [cases where faculty were denied tenure because of poor teaching], however, I believe that a distinguished publication record would have offset poor student ratings, while I seriously doubt that the reverse would be true. Good teaching "only" enhances the prof's reputation with a few students, while good research enhances the national, perhaps international, reputation of the researcher and the institution. Fortified by the knowledge that there are almost no formal penalties for bad teaching once hired, many potentially good teachers neglect this part of their work.
>
> Publications are easier to measure than teaching ability. They can be counted, but teaching ability cannot be measured by counting anything, certainly not graduate students. Actually, the more popular the teacher, the more likely he or she will be suspected of that unpardonable sin coddling. I've known of instances where junior faculty have been warned against acquiring the reputation of being a top-notch teacher or, even worse, a student advocate. (Hawley 1993, 25)

Austin, too, notes the negative effect an institutional research agenda has on teaching (1990):

> [I]n many colleges and university, an overemphasis on research as a criteria for reward ignores realities of heavy teaching loads and increasing numbers of students requiring special assistance. (68)

While the need for good teaching is increasing, the university emphasis on research is likely to take precedence when a faculty member must sort out personal work priorities. By privileging the researcher over the teacher, institutions actually encourage faculty to pay more attention to their research than to their teaching and their students.

Nor is poor teaching the only result of widespread research mania. When research productivity and reputation/rank are its dominant values, an institution will go to great lengths, and invest great resources, to attract renowned researchers—often promising them the venerated status of "non-teacher" described by Kerr (in Hawley 1993, 24). Conrad and Eagen describe the competition for such researchers (1989):

Many well-endowed colleges and universities recruit star faculty aggressively. They often lure these stars from their home institutions with high salaries, low teaching loads, first-rate faculties, and even jobs for their spouses. Faculty raiding is on the increase across the country, observes Vice President Larry Palmer of Cornell University: "We're coming after their people, they're coming after our people ... everyone is jockeying." The president of George Mason University refers to highstakes faculty recruitment as "selective development," a strategy that has netted his institution 35 top scholars in the past five years. . . .

There are both positive and negative consequences for institutional quality associated with this star search . . . But the potential drawbacks of this "free agent" approach to faculty recruitment are often overlooked. Salary inequities and privileged treatment can disrupt collegial attitudes and dispirit faculty. Teaching and service may effectively take a back seat to research. In turn, the needs of students and community become secondary. (7)

Large salaries for a few professors who teach little inevitably means more students taught by other instructors—graduate students, adjuncts, or resentful and poorly paid junior faculty. What can students expect in the classroom and faculty office when there are no institutional rewards for good professor/student interaction and no reason for instructors to feel any honor associated with being in charge of a classroom?

Indeed, the over-reliance on graduate students to teach undergraduate classes is one of the most contemptible practices in graduate schools of education today. As already noted, graduates students have successfully unionized, for the same reasons that other groups have done so: they could no longer tolerate being severely unpaid and sorely overworked. In general, the graduate teaching assistant can take one of two roads: teach well and delay making progress toward the degree, or teach poorly and insist on concentrating time and energy on the degree. Neither is a desirable option, and if so many resources weren't invested into so few research "stars," graduate students would not be routinely placed in this untenable position.

The Culture of the Professoriate

Since the culture of the academy as an organization has embraced research as its highest value, and since the research university has become the model for institutions of all types, a stress on research in professorial culture is no surprise. Professors—surely influenced by the reward and value structures of specific institutions and of the academy as a whole—generally place a high value on research activity:

> [A key value of academic culture] is the notion that the purpose of higher education is to pursue, discover, produce, and disseminate knowledge, truth, and understanding. Research, writing, publication, and instruction are all vehicles for enacting this value. (Austin 1990, 62)

As discoverers and purveyors of new knowledge and truths, professors tend to see research and publication as their worthiest tasks. Other values certainly appear in cultural rhetoric—autonomy and academic freedom, intellectual honesty and fairness, collegiality and service for society—but given the academy's drive for reputation and status, such values are commonly discounted when they conflict with a research agenda (Austin 1990, 62). Two of these values that are most commonly discounted are teaching (again) and intellectual honesty and fairness.

Concern for good teaching recurs repeatedly in this text and won't be belabored here. Instead, a comment from Austin (1990) will suffice as discussion:

> Since the various cultures that influence faculty have some conflicting values (different emphases on teaching and research, for example), an individual faculty member faces a variety of choices concerning how to allocate his or her time and effort. Furthermore, institutions often send mixed signals about what is valued; for example, institutional leaders may assert that both research and teaching are institutional priorities, but in actual practice tenure decisions depend almost solely on research contributions. In my own interviews of junior faculty in more than thirty universities, conducted among those who participated in a faculty development program focused on the enhancement of teaching, I frequently have heard this concern about mixed signals expressed. Such double messages are confusing and discouraging. (71)

If faculty have difficulty with mixed messages, how much more difficult is the choice for graduate teaching assistants, who often assume teaching responsibilities for a research-intensive department?

In examining attrition among graduate humanities students, Golde (1998) found that some students actually opt out of programs when they come to understand how teaching is devalued in practice:

Students also reported having their expectations about the faculty life slashed. Many became history students because they desired to emulate the faculty members who had excited them about the study of history. They wanted to become great teachers and interest others as they had their interest kindled. Instead, they learned that research was the important emphasis in faculty lives, a value that was communicated to graduate students. Students were advised not to put too much time into their teaching, nor to expect that teaching would be central in their future lives as faculty. (61)

The effect of a research-oriented professorial culture on graduate students, then, is sometimes to drive those most interested in becoming good teachers out of a program entirely.

What happens to others, who stay but cannot manage to shortchange their teaching responsibilities as advised? What happens to their own work and progress toward a degree? The following student report is typical:

> When I first came here, the first semester, I was asked to teach at another site and I was teaching nine credits, which as a fourth week graduate student I really thought was a bit much but I didn't know who to complain to or if I should complain. . . . Plus I was driving an hour there and an hour back and, well, figure in that I had to do two hours of office hours and then the driving three times a week. It took up all of my time. Plus a lot of correcting assignments that I had no control over because the syllabus was handed to me. And then the place was a lion's den politically. The on-site faculty member was mad at the institution because they were so controlling about the course, so he sat in and insisted I couldn't use videos I was supposed to use to limit my lecture time, and so I ended up doing a lot more lecturing and preparing for lectures than I should have. I just had no time for anything else.

While such unfair and exploitive teaching assignments are indefensible, they are only one element of ethical erosion that results from overemphasis on research and reputation.

Unhappily, a decline in ethical behavior, in intellectual honesty and fairness, has been made obvious in a range of scandals, including political, economic, sexual, and intellectual. Martin Anderson offers the fol-

Institutional Cultures and Power

lowing description of an element of professorial culture that goes widely unremarked but that is nonetheless far too common (1996):

> It is not that [professors] have lost their values, although it may be easy enough to draw this conclusion when you step back and look at some of the things they have done. No, they have values, often strong, deeply held values. The problem is that they see their values as superior ones, of a higher order than the values of ordinary people. And, if there is ever a clash between their values and the more common values of society, they will follow their own without blinking, without a trace of remorse.
>
> It is possible for them to commit acts that, cumulatively, most people would see as a loss of integrity but which they see as entirely justified and moral within their system of higher-ordered values. The reasoning goes like this: I am smarter, therefore I am better, what I believe is right is right. (129)

This climate has any number of practical implications. The numbers didn't come out right in some research? Well, then, the professor can just mend them a bit—because, after all, the hypothesis is likely to be correct (because the researcher is so smart) even if this particular study didn't work out as planned.

> While [professors] won't violate professional and ethical standards for personal monetary gain, they will violate them for other baubles. The things that academic intellectuals have such rapacity for seem to fall into three categories. The first and foremost is personal prestige and reputation, something which can be gained only by research and writing, something they will figuratively kill for. This leads to what we might call professional corruption, breaking the rules for personal prestige and reputation. We have seen how they will shirk their teaching responsibilities to get more time for research and writing. We have seen how they will go to great lengths to inflate citations counts to gain recognition for their published work. Some become desperate enough to go further. If they can't think of something worthy of publication they will plagiarize, steal the words of someone else. A few won't even bother to steal, they will simply engage in fraud, making up whatever they need. (M. Anderson 1996, 131)

A researcher out of ideas may easily *borrow* an idea from a graduate student who uncovers a fascinating new line of research. The temptation for such intellectual theft is great because the graduate student has little power and poses no threat to the faculty member. Again, the following student remark is typical:

> Everyone in my department knew about being careful not to let our advisor know about our ideas before we'd pretty much developed them by ourselves. One woman had come up with some really interesting things in her work, had laid out some really interesting directions and discussed them at length at one of our seminars. The next time she attended a public lecture by our advisor, she was stunned to hear a paraphrase of her own presentation coming out of the advisor's mouth—without any suggestion that the ideas came originally from a student, of course. We all knew about this incident and tried to keep our ideas to ourselves as long as we could. The advisor's past, we know now, is littered with people who accuse her of stealing their ideas to advance her own reputation without giving them any credit at all. But who's going to stop her? She's a star. Who'd believe us? Better yet: who'd care? (I.)

Facing such potential theft as well as heavy—and devalued—teaching responsibilities, graduate students are in a situation far removed from the supportive and mentoring atmosphere they may have expected. Too often, they serve faculty instead, as instruments used to advance the careers of institutional researchers.

Finally, Austin notes yet another value evident in current professorial culture that also helps explain a great deal of the conflict graduate students so often experience in their programs (1990):

> In addition to [other, traditional] core values, the academic profession, over the past four decades, increasingly has embraced a set of values based in the disciplinary culture . . . [including] the acceptance of the various academic disciplines as the best organizational structure to facilitate the pursuit of knowledge, the recognition that reputations are established through publications and involvement with national professional and scholarly associations, and the understanding that the reward system emphasizes specialization. (62–3)

Therefore, understanding professorial behavior also involves understanding the values and priorities of disciplinary culture.

The Culture of the Disciplines

Of all the cultures that influence faculty behavior, the disciplinary culture may well be the most influential. Austin (1990) labels it "the central source for a faculty member's identity" and cites B. Clarke (1985) to demonstrate the resulting faculty zeal:

> "Disciplines and subject specialties are going concerns in their own right, each developing in time a tradition, a social organization, a reward system, and especially an offering of professional status and dignity. Once internalized, a subject becomes an inner faith." (64–65)

Smith, in fact, believes that it is ultimately the disciplinary culture that does most to shape professorial behavior (1990):

> The loyalty of the average professor is not to his students or to the institution that employs him but to his department and, even more deeply, to his "field," for it is his field, or the scholars in his field, who ultimately validate him as a scholar and, indeed, a worthy person. (138)

One common result of disciplinary partisanship is that various departments feel superior to and frequently snub others. A psychology department, for example, might not speak to the natural science division because natural scientists believe that knowledge in the discipline of psychology is inferior (Chaffee & Tierney, 1998, 20). For a student with interests in more than one area, political problems frequently arise. Professors in one department are often scornful of those in other departments; social scientists characterize natural scientists as smug, narrow-minded and self-deceived, while natural scientists describe social scientists as "fluffy, feel-good-but-know-nothings." A student who wants to work behind the lines on the two different fronts is likely to get caught in departmental crossfire.

In addition to interdisciplinary squabbles, the specialization mandated by disciplinary zeal leads to still other problems. Experts in increasingly specialized fields become more and more knowledgeable about a smaller and smaller area. As they come to know more and more about less and less, such experts are increasingly blind to anything outside their limited perspective. In fact, Lichtman depicts specialty experts as "'scholar-researchers who more closely resemble idiot-savants than men of wisdom'" (in Smith 1990, 139). This hardly bodes well for the students who rely on the experts to explain their fields intelligibly. Moreover,

> the power of the disciplinary culture in recent years has forced splits between faculty at different ranks; junior faculty, for example, sometimes feel they must meet more stringent publication requirements to receive tenure than those faced by their senior colleagues. (Austin 1990, 68)

Resentful junior faculty facing stringent publishing demands are unlikely to take time and interest to be good mentors to graduate students; meanwhile, senior and star faculty are rewarded by having fewer and fewer responsibilities for working with students in any fashion. Where are graduate students to find good mentors, and how are they to develop any "big picture" understanding of their subject area? And, if a graduate student intends an interdisciplinary focus, it is sure to entail uphill battles involving faculty who see themselves not as colleagues but as adversaries or competitors. However much the AAU may laud graduate students for getting the faculty in different disciplines to sit down and talk together, those occasions are too often difficult and dangerous for the students themselves.

Such fragmentation makes both academic and social life difficult for students, as the following biology student notes. In one department:

> [T]here is a struggle between the older, more animal-focused faculty and the newer, more cellular-focused people. I hear much of the faculty gossip, and have heard my advisor and others complaining bitterly about feeling threatened. Our department chair doesn't help. He seems to enjoy the fighting, and pours oil on the flames periodically. . . . All of the older faculty are located in one building and the newer faculty in another. Naturally, our mail and all departmental announcements are delivered to the other building, so I frequently don't get my mail. (B.)

Apparently, choosing a specialty within a department (like choosing among departments) frequently amounts to taking up residence in someone's enemy camp.

Finally, conflicts among professors within a department can generate practical difficulties for students, especially those who are unaware they've been co-opted into a war they know nothing about. The following student, for example, found that in trying to round out a committee to administer comprehensive exams, nearly all professors responded to inquiries with a statement very like *"I remember you as a wonderful student and excellent contributor to class . . . but I am very busy now."* Only after the task was finished did the student come to understand this phenomena:

> I later found out that much of the "problem" was that apparently there had been expectations that when my advisor arrived at my institution she would "turn around" the program based on her previous experience and work. When she made it clear that she really wanted to do research and teach, not play administrator again (as she had in her previous institution), I was the means to get back at her for failing [the other faculty's expectations]. This gave me a very sour opinion of those professors, who were supposed to be (I thought) interested in graduate education, and in helping graduate students. I did not appreciate being the pawn in their little game. (V.)

INSTITUTIONAL CULTURES AND STUDENT EXPERIENCE

Austin (1990) cautions readers that "the fact that faculty members live and work in several different cultures creates some interesting and challenging tensions." Indeed. She also suggests that institutional leaders "should consider analyzing the mix of cultures at the particular institution" (69). This advice, which may serve administrators well, is nothing less than crucial for graduate students, who must interact with administrators, functionaries, and faculty, all of whom inhabit several cultures with individual values and rewards, and all of whom have some sort of power over student experience. Moreover, students face the dilemma of sorting out which values in which culture are rhetorical, serving only appearances, and which are in force, driving behavior and rewards. These are surely daunting tasks, especially for new students who enter the academy believing the ivory tower rhetoric of recruiting materials.

No wonder that the word "survival" appears so often in literature about graduate school. As the title of this chapter is meant to suggest, students must cautiously negotiate their interactions with multiple institutional representatives—each of whom must also individually navigate the demands of multiple cultures. It is an enterprise fraught with dangers that are most often hidden, and that sometimes appear in deadly combinations, as when students must choose between emphasizing their teaching responsibilities at the expense of their own research and writing, or vice versa. In such cases, compromises are not possible and something will be unavoidably sacrificed. At best, the student can hope to come out of such conflict with minimal damage, able to keep plodding on after a particular episode finally ends.

CHAPTER 4

Culture and Oppression
The "Other" as Graduate Student

> *In the late twentieth century we often forget that an academic "community" of necessity is a collection of diverse individuals and groups. To the extent that we divide groups between "us" and "them"—"us" being the mainstream, and "them" anyone who is not—we fall short of what we mean by community.*
> —WILLIAM TIERNEY

As earlier chapters have demonstrated, graduate students enter the academy in a relatively powerless position. They have been exposed to grandiose institutional rhetoric that often persuades them to feel lucky to be admitted to their academic communities and allowed a place on the bottom rung of the graduate ladder. In general, they are likely to remain silent and to adapt themselves to university norms. Soon, they discover they must navigate both the institutional bureaucracy and the conflicts of various groups and cultures competing for dominance there and in the larger society. Moreover, graduate students suffer relative powerlessness in relation to bureaucrats and professors. To become a graduate student, then, means entering a potentially oppressive relationship, as suggested in Chapter Two.

However, this general description of the graduate student's plight does not reflect the complexity of lived experience, where every human belongs to multiple groups and negotiates multiple cultures.

For example, Quinnan calls attention to some of the groups that he belongs to (1997):

> [E]ach of us cannot ignore the fact that our social status is largely determined by personal characteristics. In my case, the panoply of traits include being white, male, of European descent, educated, and middle class. (37)

Student experience will additionally be shaped, for example, by gender, sexual orientation, religion, age, race, ethnicity, class, and so on. Each personal characteristic, then, positions an individual within either a majority or a minority culture, and each individual can simultaneously be a member of various majority and minority groups. A gay white male, for example, would be included in a majority racial culture while simultaneously belonging to the minority culture of gay men. When a graduate student is a member of one or more minority cultures, the likelihood and forms of oppression increase. For example, one graduate advisor was heard commenting that she was tired of working with "those housewives from New Jersey." In this case, students were discounted because of a constellation of personal characteristics, none of which affect intellectual ability: gender, age, marital status, and locale.

Potential problems multiply for students who belong to one or more minority groups—or who, like the "housewives," belong to groups *perceived* to be out of some institutional mainstream, usually white, male, middle and upper-class, relatively young and probably Christian heterosexuals:

> The "isms"—sexism, racism, ageism, classism—are ubiquitous in the academy and in combination can prove culturally lethal for the nontraditional student. (Quinnan 1997, 29)

In her stance as student advocate, Hawley warns her readers (1993):

> If you are among the "non-traditional ones," a part-time student, a member of a minority culture, a first generation Ph.D.-seeker, a reentry woman, or somewhat older than your classmates, you are likely to be isolated from the communication networks used by more traditional students. These networks are important socializing agents, helping students address the political, social, emotional, and intellectual problems they are likely to encounter on the way to the doctorate. (5)

Such fragmentation and isolation make a difficult situation even more difficult by hindering connection between an isolated student and possible support networks, thereby increasing the student's risk of failure.

In fact, Astin (1982) found that dropout rates among minority students at each "transitional point" in the higher education pipeline, including graduate and professional schools, are "substantially higher than those for whites"; these rates were most pronounced for Hispanics and Native Americans. Astin concluded that these "leakage points" predict a future worsening of the "grossly underrepresented" status of blacks and other minorities in academic and professional circles (in Willie, Grady & Hope 1991, 23).

While success is uncertain for all graduate students, it is particularly so for those students who are also members of one or more minority cultures. To say this, however, is to say little. What exactly accounts for the increasing difficulty—the increased oppression—suffered by minority students? How is it accomplished? How is power manifested in relation to minorities? With what results? And, how do we explain minority oppression at a time when every institution has adopted affirmative action policies and identifies a support service for every imaginable group? The answer lies in a closer look at forms of oppression common to graduate study.

FORMS OF OPPRESSION

Many believe that oppression results only from intentional acts of one group having dominance over another. Emphasis on intent, however, creates a misconception that needs to be corrected before any detailed discussion of oppressive practice. Often, those involved in maintaining an oppressive relationship are the least aware of the patterns in their lived experience:

> [O]ppression is the inhibition of a group through a vast network of everyday practices, attitudes, assumptions, behaviors, and institutional rules; it is structural or systemic. The systemic character of oppression implies that an oppressed group need not have a correlate oppressing group. While structural oppression in our society involves relations among groups, these relations do not generally fit the paradigm of one group's consciously and intentionally keeping another down.... The conscious actions of many individuals daily contribute to maintaining and reproducing oppression, but those people are usually simply doing their jobs or living their lives, not understanding themselves as agents of oppression. (Young 1992, 180–81)

It is not that one group works to keep another in submission; instead, "for every oppressed group there is a group that is *privileged* in relation to [it]"—and majority groups rarely recognize their own privilege (Young 181).

Because such privilege is often unrecognized and unremarked, it is perhaps best revealed through experiences of minority groups who lack it. Critical theorists and researchers use the concept of "Otherness" when contrasting the experiences of majority/non-majority groups. In brief, Otherness is "a unique concept alluding to the cultural remoteness of any disadvantaged population (e.g., ethnic minorities, women, older persons)" (Quinnan 1997, 16). While, like other students, the Other is likely to enter the institution believing it to be an idealistic haven, he or she finds instead what Quinnan terms "xenophobic culture and customs" (1997, 3). The following four forms of oppression are common among groups perceived as Other, and once defined, they will be demonstrated in the experiences of several non-mainstream groups: women, students of color, older students, lesbian/gays, and working class students.

Before moving on to these sections, however, we wish to emphasize this point: our intensive focus on minority experience here is *not* meant to suggest that majority students don't suffer these injustices. *All* graduate students are threatened by these mechanisms. But while it's true that no group is safe, it's also true that some groups will experience them in greater intensity and frequency than others. For example, while any student might have difficulty securing a sympathetic advisor, marginalized students are more likely to have difficulty finding an advisor affiliated with their race or sexual orientation—certainly not the case for heterosexual whites. We choose to discuss forms of oppression in relation to the minority experience, then, because minority experience offers the most inclusive picture and most telling examples of these routine oppressive mechanisms.

Marginalization

The term *marginal* applies to any group designated the Other and suggests a location on the fringes of some society. It is important to understand, however, that this marginalized location still falls within the community of the institution.

> [T]he social structure as a whole does not "expel," nor is marginal man a "being outside of." He is, on the contrary, a "being inside of," within the social structure, and in a dependent relationship. . . . they are "beings for another." (Freire 1985, 48)

The institution needs students, and it needs to be able to claim fairness and egalitarianism; in this sense the graduate student Other serves institutional needs. Indeed, what is particularly insidious about marginalization

Culture and Oppression

in the academy is that an institution can appear democratic and inclusive by admitting non-mainstream students while actually safeguarding established privilege by discriminating against them. That is, once inside the academy they find themselves treated less preferentially than mainstream, privileged groups. They may, for example, have more difficulty getting access to faculty, having their work taken seriously, or securing funding to support their studies.

Exploitation

Exploitation occurs whenever a privileged group enjoys increased power, status, and wealth from the work and energy of others. For example, the individual efforts of non-mainstream students become institutional capital when the institution touts its diversity enrollment figures; x number of minorities = x amount of prestige and goodwill for the university. Whatever the student's reason for studying at a particular institution, and regardless of his or her progress, the institution exploits its Other populations by bragging about their presence on campus.

There is also, however, a sense in which individual students experience exploitation much more personally. Attempting to define a type of exploitation that applies more specifically to a variety of minority groups (women, for example), Young (1992) proposes that we think in terms of menial work, which she characterizes in part as:

> low-paying work lacking in autonomy, and in which a person is subject to orders from several people. Menial work tends to be auxiliary work, instrumental to another person's work, in which that other person receives primary recognition for doing the job. (185)

Of course, all research and teaching assistantships generally fit this description, but the more a student needs money, the less choice he or she has about work conditions. Discriminated against in the society at large, non-mainstream students frequently enter the academy with greater financial need than the more privileged majority. In this sense, the Other is often more subject to exploitation than more mainstream groups.

Powerlessness

Why discuss powerlessness in relation to minority graduate students or the Other when, in reality, this whole text is essentially about power in the academy—who has it, who does not—and its effects? It's also true that all grad students lack power to some extent. For the Other, however, the experience of powerlessness is compounded. Furthermore, in these days while the academy is shouting for diversity, inclusion, multiculturalism, curriculum reform, and more, at its core it is acting in ways that contradict its rhetoric. Attention must be paid.

Powerlessness, of course, refers to being in a situation—real or perceived—where one cannot affect the course of events, particularly in relation to one's own life. People do what they do because they believe they have no choice, which is the case in instances of situated power (see Chapter 2). Young suggests expanding this definition by including, among other factors, the right to "participate in making decisions that regularly affect the conditions of their lives and actions" and the right to respect (Young 1992, 189).

Again, this general description—a sense of being unable to affect events, of being excluded from decision-making, and of routinely being denied respect—applies to all graduate students in some ways. No student, for example, enjoys the respect that professors do. However, neither do women enjoy the respect accorded to men, nor do older students enjoy the respect accorded to their younger colleagues. Powerlessness, then, is another disadvantage that intensifies for the Other in the academy.

Violence

Most readers would assume they know a "violent" act when they see one. But, to uncover the nature and extent of violence threatening the Other, it's necessary to explicitly define the nature of what Young calls "systematic and legitimized violence" against minority groups (1992):

> The members of some groups live with the fear of random, unprovoked attacks on their persons or property, which have no motive but to damage, humiliate, or destroy them.... Violation may also take the form of name-calling or petty harassment intended to degrade or humiliate, and always signals an underlying threat of physical attack.... Such violence is systematic because it is directed at any member of the group simply because he or she is a member of that group. (193–194)

Included as an act of violence, then, is any harassing act based on minority group status because it implies the possibility of a physical attack.

These forms of oppressive mechanisms—marginalization, exploitation, powerlessness, and violence—are common within the framework

Culture and Oppression

of graduate education, but a more detailed analysis of minority students' graduate experiences reveals how instances of oppression multiply for some students.

EXPERIENCE OF THE OTHER

Women Students

Writing about the difficulties women experience as they pursue a Ph.D., Levstik (1982) offers this pointed advice: "If you want marriage, children, and a Ph.D. it is best to be an heiress. Second best is to marry rich" (96). And for women, the difficulties of time and work management Levstik discusses are perhaps the least of their challenges. As a marginalized group in a dominant male society, women are far less likely to earn a doctorate. Instead, they often become victims of constructed male consciousness and discrimination and become not only powerless and silent in relation to men, but also subject to severe exploitation.

Despite a prevailing perception in society at large that women have finally achieved equity with men, statistics indicate that they are still vastly underrepresented as holders of prestigious doctorates.

> While the total number of both men and women earning the Ph.D. has increased in the last 20 years, women's proportionate share has remained at 35 percent from 1986 until 1989 when their numbers increased one percentage point. (Hawley 1993, 10)

This statistic, demonstrating that two men earn doctorates for every one woman, is bad enough—but it's actually still worse than it appears on the surface. Hanson (1992) reports that during the period of time that would produce this 1:2 ratio, there were actually *more* women than men enrolled in doctoral programs: 758,624 women compared with 673,314 men (8).

Not only do women earn only slightly more than a third of all doctorates awarded despite their enrollment in large percentages, but the degrees they do earn take longer and promise fewer returns on their investment. In general, it takes women 27 percent longer to complete their degrees, a factor which may well be related to the fact that they are less likely than men to receive financial help during graduate study (Hawley 1993). And, even when they do succeed, women are likely to find that they earn less money than a man with the same degree.

While women have made some gains in such fields as math and science, where they have been traditionally underrepresented, Hawley reports that

> Nevertheless, women are still behind in these fields (18% in physical sciences, and 8% in engineering). . . . The 1990 report also shows that education is the only broad field in which women outnumber men, comprising 58% of the earned doctorates. (Hawley 1993, 10)

Perhaps it is no accident that the one area in which women receive more degrees than men is education, traditionally "women's work" and one of the lowest paid professions. And, given Levstik's observations about women's responsibilities outside the classroom and their financial difficulties, perhaps it is no accident that education is also the field with the longest time-to-degree—an average of almost eighteen years, more than twice as long as the physical sciences' shortest time of 7.6 years (10). Moreover, education is usually the department least funded and least respected in universities.

Women, then, tend to be ghettoized in generally poorly regarded departments of education. If they should happen to find their way into other areas, like science, they often subsequently find themselves steered into and contained in an "appropriate" specialty. In 1994, for example, while women earned only some 20 percent of doctorates in most areas of math and science, they earned 41 percent of degrees in biology and the life sciences (Sanders, Koch & Urso 1997, 6). It is hard to imagine that so many women just somehow *happen* to like the least-respected and least-rewarding field without some kind of institutional manipulation.

Women, like all students, are inevitably influenced by what they experience after entering the academy, a bastion of male power and privilege:

> A successful socialization process is critical for a successful graduate career. Historically, the socialization of graduate students has been controlled by the prevailing culture which, until rather recently, has been overwhelmingly white and almost exclusively male. Acculturation has been generally most successful for those who could fit the status quo most comfortably. (Turner & Thompson 1993, 357)

No wonder, then, that acculturation and success are less likely for women than men. They needn't do more than look around them to understand who holds the power of the institution: "Another glance sideways reveals that the majority of adjuncts, lecturers, and composition faculty

Culture and Oppression

are women; tenured and tenure-track faculty are men" (Tokarczyk & Fay 1993, 16). Obviously, women labor in the tenuous, low-paying positions while their male counterparts enjoy the high-paying secure positions.

In an atmosphere that so obviously privileges men over women, the women students often display just the sort of constructed consciousness that supports their oppression:

> [One] barrier that seems to impact women is the negative perception they have of themselves as scholars. Adler (1976) indicates that "women seem to share with men the belief that females are less competent and perhaps less able to undertake or succeed at professional work than are males" . . . [said one female Ph.D. candidate] At times I felt as if someday "they" would find out that I was not really intellectually capable. (Hanson 1992, 10).

In addition to signals from institutional materials suggesting that any entrant may well prove unworthy (see Chapter 2), women suffer the additional strain of enculturation by a society that remains largely sexist despite decades of feminist activism.

Feeling out of place in a competitive male environment, women are among those who feel most silenced in the classroom,

> allowing their own voices and questions to be swallowed in the presence of fellow students. It is not until the class breaks into small groups, where the men sit silent, that the women speak up. (Tokarcyk & Fay 1993, 16)

So it isn't that women have nothing to say, it's that classroom pedagogies often run counter to women's natural ways of working.

Not only are their professors most likely to be men, but to be men who are not much impressed by women students and who are likely to discriminate against them. No matter where they made an academic home, women are generally

> vociferous and almost unanimous in reporting passive gender discrimination in their programs—a sense of being passed over in favor of less able male students—in every major. (Turner & Thompson 1993, 364)

It is unlikely that this sense of discrimination is imagined; Bolig (1982), for example, reports "overt and covert labeling by faculty of women Ph.D. students as 'less committed,' 'less likely to complete' and 'less likely to be productive' than male Ph. D. students" (22). In the almost twenty years since Bolig wrote about attitudes towards women, nothing much has changed. Today reports from women students are full of anecdotes reflecting such discrimination, often intensified by their membership in more than one institutional minority:

> I always felt an outsider—as a female, then as a married student, someone from the East and a city, as an ecologist in a field of growing molecular biology—I fought feelings of being an imposter or not conforming. . . . The feelings of being an outsider were pushed under, and they still affect my feelings of belonging and self worth. (L.)

> At one graduate school "recruiting visit" I attended, it became noticeable that my prospective advisor had an affiliative relationship with his male students and a distant and uncomfortable relationship with his female students. When I told a male graduate student at that school that not only did I feel that the prospective advisor seemed uncomfortable around me personally, but I also noticed a 'sex difference' in the advisor's interpersonal relationships, the graduate student said it was an unfortunate personal problem of his and recommended that if I wanted to be treated as an equal to male students, I should choose a different program. Needless to say, I did. (A.)

It is interesting to note the rhetoric of the grad student in the quote above. The student thinks that the "unfortunate personal problem" is an idiosyncratic problem of the advisor and not a problem with the power structure of the institution. This student's need to change programs was echoed in other interviews we conducted.

Perhaps the most severe of all dangers for women in the university is sexual harassment.

> The power a professor holds over a student, especially a graduate student pursuing an advanced degree, can be difficult to imagine for anyone who has not been in that position. Depending on how badly the student wants a grade or a degree in order to pursue a lifelong dream, the professor's power can approach that exercised by a warden over a prisoner, by a master over a slave. Nothing so gross as a physical threat or force is necessary; the threat to one's career carries equivalent weight. (Anderson, M. 1996, 157–158)

Any professor who can withhold an assistantship or assign a failing grade can shut a student out of access to department resources. Therefore any professor has a powerful grip on students in his or her charge. Of course, men can also suffer sexual harassment by professors of either gender, but rarely are women professors charged with assaulting male students. That is not, however, the case for male professors assaulting female students:

> Studies more than confirm what has long been suspected. In the university world dominated and controlled by males, the female student is substantially at risk. . . . . [In a 1985 paper presented to the American Psychological Association], the authors reported that "of 246 women graduate students in their sample, 12.7 percent indicated they had been sexually harassed, 21 percent had not enrolled in a course to avoid such behavior . . . 2.6 percent dropped a course because of it, and 15.9 percent indicated that they had been directly assaulted." (Anderson, M. 1996, 159)

Moreover, when an academic is accused and found guilty of such assaults, often the institutional response is to cover up the incident and protect both itself and the perpetrator. "Star" faculty who have assaulted women have subsequently been given paid leaves and institutional awards in such revered institutions as Harvard, Yale, Emory, and Princeton (Anderson, M. 1996, 160–166). Women, then, find their academic options narrowed and their bodies threatened because of institutional hubris and male privilege.

Students of Color

> Like women, students of color are clear numerical minorities in graduate schools. It is a commonplace that most minority groups are poorly represented among doctoral recipients. In 1988, blacks received 3.9 percent of all doctorates awarded to U.S. residents in all fields of study; Hispanics received 2.9 percent; Asians received 5.1 percent; and whites received the remaining 88.1 percent. (Bowen & Rudenstine 1992, 37)

Also like women, black students tend to be clustered in certain subject areas, one of which is education.

> [B]lacks are relatively heavily represented in professional fields, in education, and in the more policy-relevant social sciences; of the 951

doctorates received by blacks in 1988, over 400 were in education. In our six arts-and-sciences fields, the percentages of doctorates received by blacks ranged from a low of 0.8 percent in mathematics to 1.6 percent in physics, 1.8 percent in history, 3.2 percent in economics, 4.2 percent in English and American literature, and a high of 7.1 percent in political science and public policy. (Bowen & Rudenstine 1992, 37)

While education is certainly a field worth studying, again it is worth noticing that it is a poorly paid profession—and over 40 percent of all black students earn doctorates in that area. This statistic is particularly thought-provoking given the conclusion drawn in Alexander Astin's 1982 study of persistence among black graduate and professional students: " higher education serves as a principal gate keeper for entry into the most prestigious and lucrative careers" (Willie, Grady & Hope 1991, 23).

In addition, students of color on predominantly white college campuses experience both isolation and discrimination, as well as a sense of being on trial (Willie, Grady & Hope 1991, 50) as do women. Not only do minority scholars have less access to faculty mentors than white students, but they receive less financial support. Willie, Grady & Hope (1991) report the following in a major study of African-American doctoral experience.

> The greatest areas of dissatisfaction for these black students at predominantly white graduate schools were the lack of opportunities to engage in collaborative work with faculty and the absence of racial diversity of the faculty ... [including] opportunities to serve as teaching and research assistants. ... The white graduate scholars had easy access to their teachers and often were chosen as teaching assistants. This was not the experience of black scholars on such campuses. ... (52, 59)

This report includes findings from others that also demonstrate that "whites are more likely to be awarded fellowships and graduate teaching assistantships" and that black students are "excluded from access to full participation in federal contracts and grants awarded to predominantly white institutions" (27). And, when African Americans are awarded funding, it is frequently inadequate:

> A majority of the scholars required more than 5 years to obtain their degrees. Yet most received their final grants the fourth year of study or earlier. ... By not making funds available to African-American scholars beyond the fourth year of graduate study, granting agencies place

such students and their investments in them at risk. Data from this study suggest that some students may never complete their degrees because of the combined pressures of increased family responsibilities and diminished financial assistance. (40)

Not only do students of color receive less support from faculty and campus organizations, but they also have fewer opportunities to fund their studies. All of these factors amount to roadblocks.

Comments from students of color reflect the oppression they experience especially when they understand how they are used to serve the university's ends:

> I received an application to one university which I had not considered or researched. This institution provided a waiver of its application fee to me because they received my name off the GRE Minority Locator service. Surprisingly, this same institution called me personally to try to recruit me. I was flown to the university campus for a visit . . . Once I was there, I found the environment welcoming because a faculty [member] of color, from the same ethnic background as myself, met with me and took me out to dinner. She showed me around the campus and encouraged me to attend this institution. I was sold. . . .
>
> I didn't feel like I belonged there once I began my first semester. The administrative staff in my department was not very friendly or helpful. They were not patient with me and seemed bothered by questions they assumed I should know the answers to. I also felt tokenized. Faculty that I met commented that I was the Native American applicant. I felt under pressure and also stigmatized because I got a sense that some thought I was admitted due to my ethnic status.
>
> I began to question my ability to pursue graduate studies. I thought that maybe I was admitted to fill some kind of quota or to be a token for the department. At the time, I was the only Native American in the program. I felt a lot of pressure to excel beyond what my peers were doing to prove to myself and the department that I could hold my own. It was difficult as well because there were not any Native American faculty in my program. There was only one woman of color as well. It left me feeling like I chose the wrong place to be.
>
> As part of the package for my acceptance to the program, I was told that I would have a graduate assistantship position. The

faculty member who promised this to me started sabbatical leave that semester. For whatever reason, the position that was promised to me was given to another student. Therefore, I was without a job until October. This was particularly difficult because my husband was still in our hometown working and would not be moving with me until January. Keeping up two apartments was a hardship without the financial support from the institution. I did receive a tuition waiver, but the stipend from the job would have made things much easier my first semester. (S.)

For this student, the minority experience included a major initiative to recruit her involving a female professor of color, the only one at the institution. But it also included treatment as a token, the sense of being on trial and having to outperform white counterparts, and loss of financial support promised by the university. Perhaps instead of asking why so few minorities earn doctorates, we should ask how so many manage to do so given this kind of treatment.

Because belonging to more than one minority group tends to intensify Otherness and resulting discrimination, women of color are at an especially severe disadvantage. In addition to suffering the disadvantages of color, they also suffer the disadvantages of gender. When compared to white women, they do worse as a group than their white counterparts as Turner and Thompson point out in their 1993 study.

> More majority women had apprenticeship and mentoring experiences. More frequently they reported the presence of support networks inside their departments. . . . In general, majority women participating in this study had more opportunities than women of color for such apprenticeship opportunities as research and teaching assistantships, coauthoring papers with a faculty member, making presentations at professional conferences, and being introduced by faculty to a network of influential academics who could provide support for students seeking entry-level jobs. . . . Thus, we can conclude that minority women have less opportunity for successful academic careers. (360, 365)

Specifically only 49 percent of minority women held assistantships while 60 percent of majority women did; 27 percent of minority women coauthored articles, while 52 percent of the majority women did (Turner & Thompson 1993, 360). Minority women's chances for success are even more limited than for their majority counterparts.

There seems little doubt that minority women suffer from the dominant culture of white males, especially regarding opportunities controlled by primarily male professors. Turner and Thompson (1993), citing Blackwell, outline the ways minority women may be marginalized by white, male professors.

> [t]hose who teach are often guilty of subconscious (though sometimes conscious and deliberate) efforts to reproduce themselves through students they come to respect, admire, and hope to mentor. As a result, mentors tend to select as proteges persons who are of the same gender and who share with themselves a number of social and cultural attributes or background characteristics such as race, ethnicity, religion, and social class. Because minorities are presently underrepresented in faculty positions, such practices inevitably result in the underselection of minorities as proteges. (367)

Having a mentor can make a student's path through the university much smoother. Because faculty frequently choose students like themselves to mentor and since most faculty are white, opportunities for mentors are extremely limited for students out of the mainstream.

Again, it isn't hard to recognize oppression born of being both female and of color in the firsthand accounts of women students:

> [My advisor had] a huge ego and a gutter mouth. I suffered as a result of this. He was arrogant and rude to me right off the bat. I'm fundamentally shy around people I don't know real well, and it was hard for me to shut up and put up, but I felt like I didn't have a choice. . . . The music department at this school is so small and this university is SO WHITE. I'm biracial with a British schooling background. . . . It's hard to be a minority in a very white program because people look at you funny. They are more likely to see your "diversity" interests as strange. I wanted to do research in women composers but [my advisor] pooh-poohed it as a topic that wouldn't get my dissertation approved or get me a job.
>
> These professors a lot of times can get so wrapped up in their male-oriented, white world, that they don't understand that non-white students are different. We think differently, we view things differently, and you can't just approach a non-white student the exact same way as white students who grew up in this country. (N.)

The catalogue of forms of oppression in just this brief anecdote are many: verbal/sexual harassment through profanity; lack of respect;

powerlessness; marginalization; discrimination. . . . If all women need, as Levstik (1982) suggests, to be wealthy, women of color need not only money but also a great deal more perseverance and tolerance than their white counterparts.

Older Students

Increasingly, students who complete their baccalaureate degrees work for several years before beginning graduate study. As a result, a larger and larger segment of the graduate population has become representative of students who might be considered at or near middle age. Their age and experience contrasts with the traditional graduate student who enters immediately upon completing a baccalaureate. Quinnan (1997) asks:

> If indeed adults comprise a new subculture in the extremely rigid, change-resistant environment that is academe, are their voices, perspectives, and experiences assigned a value similar to the dominant group? Or are they . . . equated with Otherness (Giroux 1990), a nameless, faceless attribute forced upon disadvantaged groups different from the majority because of race, ethnicity, gender, class or age? (33)

Not only Quinnan's study but narratives from students offer evidence that like women and students of color, older students are also designated Other and marginalized in graduate programs.

The bureaucracy that shows so little respect to students in general seems obstinately unaware that adults might merit any particular consideration.

> Part of my sense of being an outsider was that I am the only single parent in the graduate program. My ability to attend social functions that help forge mentor relationships was limited. And I was so busy learning to be a Teaching Assistant, and completing my coursework and parenting that I had no energy left to do the extra things that students get rewarded for here (being on committees, doing certain volunteer work). Being a single parent at this graduate school is rare. I am being judged and rewarded as though I were 23 with no children, no aging parents, no responsibilities other than academic. My attitude and progress have been impeded because I have been judged as not being one of the best and the brightest simply because I have more to do, more to

accomplish, more to contend with that is non-academic than my peers. (Y.)

Whatever their talents in the classroom, adults are expected to behave like unencumbered young adults outside it. If they don't, they pay an academic penalty.

Moreover, despite years of responsibility and life experience, older students are treated like youngsters and are expected to act and sound just like their junior colleagues. Weiland (1998) reports that when Rosa Maria Pegueros returned to graduate school after completing a law degree and spending ten years in social work,

> Her first and chief disappointment was being treated as a child, "infantilized" as she puts it, when professors and administrators alike could not recognize what her experience had already supplied to her emerging vocation. "I came back to school as a confident adult, secure in my ability to manage a life balanced between work and love, only to have my priorities questioned and even displaced by a profession that places little importance on being a successful *person*." (23)

How is it that the academy is so quick to discount a person's previous success elsewhere?

Several researchers suggest that the answer, in part, is that adult students pose a potential threat to the status quo:

> [A]dults quickly learn that universities welcome them as long as their usual ways of operating do not have to make accommodation (Reissman 1980). Where older students find the going becomes more treacherous is in raising challenges to bureaucratic structures and attitudes designed for younger, less sophisticated counterparts. With life experience in testing boundaries, adults are a potential threat to the authority and autonomy of the academy by virtue of their unwillingness to abide by the status quo (Karol & Ginsburg 1980). Because they use this experience base critically to assess course content, college policies, and teaching styles, adults place themselves at further risk in higher education for challenging not just the authority of the academy, but the values and beliefs—or ideology—undergirding university culture (Paterson 1979). In traditional academic cliques, adults may be viewed as invaders into the body politic (Boyer 1990), bringing with them demands that could prove an anathema to the power and prestige of those

nestled safely in the academy. In postmodern theory, adults earn "at-risk" status simply because they are culturally suspect to the established order. (Quinnan 1997, 33)

Unlike younger students who remain voiceless against the university, adult students, often in positions of authority in the real world, are more likely to question and criticize the idiosyncrasies of the academy, and therefore disturb the status quo of the institution. Students who do not conform to the university's norms are often considered "at risk" when in actuality it is the university that feels "at risk."

Many students find themselves outsiders simply because they have sufficient self-confidence to ask honest and intelligent questions.

The narrative from this student is typical:

> I came to train and acquire a Ph.D. at the age of 37. Prior to this I had run an education department for a local Planned Parenthood, chaired committees that boasted people like the mayor as members, served as the president and search committee chairperson for a local congregation. In short, I had been a person of some influence and power in my community and, as a result, had a most profound experience of authority and power structure when hitting graduate school.
>
> It isn't easy being older than most of my professors! The social norm in academia is that graduate students will immediately bond with others in their position, junior faculty will affiliate with "their own," and the senior folk are from another generation. Although I was older than ALL of the junior faculty (and possessed a self confidence that comes with age and experience that they'd yet to discover) I noticed that I occasionally freaked them out. "WHO IS THIS WOMAN who dares to ask me to defend my assertions?" "Why is she so damned confident that she can ask questions at a meeting with all the faculty that I feel too timid to ask?" (F.)

How are such self-confident students treated? Too often, they receive unmistakable signals that they are not welcome.

> I had one professor for two required theory courses that almost caused me to quit graduate school. I had a reputation of being strong in theory, and there was nothing I could say or do that

produced a positive response in her. It got to the point that other students in the class were embarrassed, and talked to me about it after class. She interrupted me, belittled me, cut me short on my presentations. My written work was quite good, and she made few comments on it, just gave me my grade. I saw what she wrote on other papers that received grades equal to or less than mine, and her comments were much more interested and supportive. While I was frustrated, I thought it was simply a personality conflict, until the next year another single mother was admitted to the program. Her experience was even worse than mine. Many times she called me in tears to figure out what to do with this particular professor. This student left the program because of how unfriendly it was to single parents. (M.)

Given the absolute power that faculty have over the fate of graduate students, they have little difficulty driving students they deem undesirable out of their programs.

As unjust as it may be to exclude students because of their self-confidence, Quinnan (1997) reports that several theorists believe there may be an even more insidious reason for the marginalization:

> Perhaps unwittingly, economist Gary Becker provides material for an answer in his *Human Capital* (1975). In a section concerning the relationship between asset appreciation and depreciation (226–228), he outlines a theoretical reply to the question of why colleges refrain from investing too heavily in the human capital of adult students. Younger students are seen as an outlay for the future. They have years of work, earnings, philanthropy, and social and financial productivity still ahead of them, all of which may be viewed as collateral on the university's investment. At the other end, adult students come to college in the "depreciating" stages of their productive years. Rosen (1975, 200) describes this decline in "people's usefulness in the economy" as functional obsolescence. (50–51)

Younger students are more likely to take on the mission of their advisers and, therefore, bring money to the university and fame to their mentors. Older students generally have their own agenda and their own life's work. They are not interested in being some else's protégé. Therefore they are marginalized and oppressed. The idea that adults are less welcome because they have less potential monetary value to the university is so crass that it might be difficult to believe—except that universities themselves, as discussed in Chapter Two, openly exploit their younger graduate students, their "best and brightest," in recruiting materials, exactly as if they were in fact corporate assets.

Despite their experiences, older students wind up like every one else. Like other marginalized groups, they are rendered silent and experience a sense of powerlessness as a result of the hostile climate they encounter. Quinnan describes the way older students yield to the power structure:

> Adult learners, quicker to develop an awareness of university methods to quell dissent, are quickly reduced to frustration in trying to reform the power structure along less vertical lines. Rather than continuing the fight against so strong a foe, they relent and resign themselves to "just getting through." To date, I cannot recall an event where adult students, properly agitated, have held protests or conducted demonstrations demanding a broader say in decisions affecting their education. They appear not to have developed the collective consciousness to act en masse for change. (Quinnan 1997, 52–53)

Even though adult students may arrive at the portals of academe with more life experience and self confidence than the younger students, their confidence and their willingness to speak up for themselves and fight the system is soon eroded.

Lesbian and Gay Students

Another group that suffers marginalization and powerlessness and overt violence as well is composed of gay, lesbian, bisexual, and transgendered (GLBT) students. Virtually every element of campus culture and climate signals outsider status and warns these students they are not wanted. Like older students, they are clearly the "outsiders" in relation to social events and they experience unconcealed discrimination from university personnel. This student, in fact, is able to identify the outsider status of both gay and older, married students.

> I continually feel that I am not a whole partner in the educational process at my program. My program puts a large deal of effort and time into facilitating the group dynamics. But I come from a different "group," so to speak. Being an out lesbian in a relation-

> ship, the social side of the program never seemed entirely open to me.... Despite the department's apparent interest in community, its plans seemed to exclude older students and those with families.... (Q.)

The following student also confronted a culture that seemed intent on denying the very existence of a GLBT population:

> During my first semester at this school, I became a member of a department support group, a group that was graduate student run and dealt with GLB issues. In the second semester, I became the co-chair of this group and when I came back for the second year, I was the chair. At the beginning of the second year, when each person in the department was asked to select a group to be part of, the description for this group stated something along the lines of "This team will deal with issues of diversity." I felt very slighted as this is not what was supposed to be said. The group had dealt with GLB issues in the past and was supposed to do that again. Upon questioning one of the associate directors for the department, I was told that they wanted to reevaluate the group. I was able to convince them that it was needed to deal the GLB issues as the school itself was homophobic and uneducated. Thankfully, others interested came forward in my support and the group dealt solely with GLB topics. But I did find that the year after I left, it was changed to a "Diversity Group" and GLB issues no longer have a front role for the department. (B.)

It appears that some institutions believe they can wish this population into oblivion.

Beyond feeling isolated, gay and lesbian students experience the campus climate as threatening:

> It was easy to tell that I didn't belong shortly after arriving. I had a rainbow flag sticker on my car bumper and felt very worried that something might happen to me or my car if I left it on there. I took the sticker off within one week of moving down there and that hurt very much. The school had a student organization made up of people in my department and while I later found out that there were two other gay members (out of 60), they were both

> closeted. My feeling like an outsider only strengthened when I heard that student affairs employees were making homophobic comments and jokes. This didn't make me feel very safe or happy to be there. (X.)

While many institutions boast of hosting numbers of students of color, none boasts of its gay and lesbian population. In these hostile climates, students find not only powerlessness and a need to be silent, but also a need to be invisible as well.

The fear of violence is realistic; the threat of violence seems heightened by the fact that the university at large generally remains silent on the matter of discrimination based on sexual orientation. Homophobic remarks are common and often socially acceptable; harassment is widespread. Although Evans and Wall (1991) do not write specifically about graduate school, they describe the university climate in which gays must function. Surveys of gay, lesbian, and bisexual students revealed that:

> Between 45 and 65% of respondents reported having experienced verbal insults, 22 to 26% reported being "followed or chased," and 12 to 15% noted they had been sexually harassed or assaulted. Threats of physical violence were reported by 16 to 25% of those surveyed, and 35 to 58% said they feared for their safety. Others experienced having objects thrown at them, having their property damaged, receiving threats of public exposure, being spat upon, and being physically assaulted with weapons. Over 90% expected to experience further acts of homophobic harassment while in college. (Berrill 1989)

Although most people are upset by these homophobic abuses, many people are not aware of the dangers that verbal slurs and name-calling pose:

> Such as off-handed jabs as "Hey you faggot!" or "What a fag!" or "She's such a dyke!" are often heard while walking among a crowd of college students or through a residence hall lobby. Most students, faculty, and staff do not understand how these seemingly innocuous comments are actually powerful oppressive tools that create and reinforce fear and contempt toward lesbians, gays, and bisexuals and remind everyone of the negative consequences for those who cross over socially approved gender role behavior. Students clearly learn the difference between acceptable and unacceptable behavior on campus when

> they hear faculty, coaches, administrators, and hall directors confront racist jokes and sexist comments but not homophobic slurs. (Evans & Wall 1991, 46)

Evans and Wall also report that most of the incidents of harrassment go unreported.

> [Students] may fear the consequences of public exposure in the campus newspaper or a violation of confidentiality. They may also want to avoid a negative response from the staff with whom they have to work throughout the reporting process. In addition, reports and rumors of acts of individual harassment and abuse may provide warnings to other bisexuals, lesbians, and gays to "stay in the closet." The threat of potential violence is an effective tool that keeps many people from living a more open lifestyle and from organizing to work in coalition to combat homophobia and heterosexism in the public arena. (Evans & Wall 1991, 46–47)

Discrimination against gay and lesbian students is implicitly condoned by universities whose culture allows it to flourish unchecked.

In addition to social discrimination and threats of violence, lesbian and gay students also frequently suffer from professorial bias against them and/or their research interests. Again, the following student reports are typical:

> In my program we have the opportunity to select a specialty area or concentration. My concentration is Diverse Populations, specifically GLBT student services/resource management. I had felt on more than one occasion that I was rocking the boat, so to speak, by selecting such a controversial area. I have felt that my research was often given that slight smile of uselessness, that my interns were not valued as much as if they were in judicial services or housing. I do not look to my faculty for any type of mentorship, I am taking more credits so that I can graduate early, and I look to other professionals for advice on my research and career goals.

> I spent five years working and then went back for my Ph.D. I did have a problem with the lack of concern they had for the gay community. I felt that a lot of my professors missed the boat.

They did not want to address any issues that pertained to the gay community. I found this disturbing because this was a counseling program and I was wondering if every time someone ran into a gay person they'd refer that person out. I mean, the counseling department had no course to help future counselors know how to address the gay community, so if someone were out getting "real world" experience, they were told to refer "out" to another professional or center. And, the sad fact is that a lot of folks in this department think that all gay people should come out or be outed. This is what I find disturbing—this total lack of understanding and disregard for individuality.

Also, my major advisor was very homophobic and when he found out what my research interest was he said I was using it as a vehicle to come out (yeah, right). The topic was homophobia in sports and its impact on women. I had to fire him and find a new advisor. This was a nightmare because now my time would be even longer in the grad program. I finally found an advisor who would take on the topic—as long as we changed the title so that it would pass through the institutional approval process. Nice: now I had to closet my research. . . .

The most interesting thing that I found during this nightmare was that my committee never wanted to talk about the subject matter homophobia; they always talked about race or women's struggles or development, but when it came down to the real part of the research they would ignore it. . . . I found it very strange that in the world of academics and research there is such a need to cover up and hide good studies. It is a shame that researchers are afraid to get labeled as gay or gay friendly if they do any kind of gay related research.

Gay and lesbian students, then, find themselves shut out of social events, silenced, physically harassed and threatened, pressured into invisibility and forced to hide or abandon their own research interests.

What impact can such oppression have on the students who experience it? This student is eloquent on that subject:

All in all, if I had to go through it again I wouldn't. Am I a better person? Not really. What did I learn? That educators talk the talk but they can't walk the walk. Will I ever let this happen to another person? Absolutely not. The academic hazing stops here. No one should give up their identity in order to have three letters after their name. What does Ph.D. stand for to me? The Power to Handle the Devil!

Working Class Students

In addition to gender, race, age, and sexual orientation, some graduate students also find themselves marginalized because of a working class background. Lack of the cultural capital that marks the middle class—speech patterns, for example—brand these students outsiders as well, and like the others they pay a price for being "different."

Like other groups, working-class students are well aware of their outsider status. Synthesizing elements of biographies written by working-class academics, Weiland (1998) says:

> Graduate students with working-class backgrounds have a keen sense of social injustice, the irony of their professional circumstances, and the everyday peculiarities of the academic vocations. (23)

That is, they know that graduate study isn't intended for them and that they are not the people gatekeepers expect to succeed. Their status is made clear by passwords and codes among dominant members of the institution that have nothing to do with academic ability and everything to do with cultural capital. As one student has said,

> "Graduate school is about more than what you know. . . . The problem isn't knowing the material in class but knowing the references made over cappuccino." (Weiland 1998, 23)

Common social backgrounds and experience are assumed, and those whose experience differs are soon exposed.

The result is as it is for other groups, as is evident in this report from a working-class academic:

> Nowhere did I feel a greater need for disguise than inside academic institutions where the heightened level of discourse both fascinated and intimidated me and put me in situations where I most feared that someone would discover that I was only pretending to be "educated" and force me to leave. Although I felt a great deal of tension, confusion, and discomfort, I was not able to articulate these feelings as linked to

class oppression. The mechanisms of a dominant discourse were fully in operation: I internalized my feelings as somehow related to something out of place or missing in me rather than as indicative of a system of oppression carefully masked by myths of equal access and opportunity.... [T]hrough my experiences of difference eventually came the knowledge that exposed the central fallacy under which all educational systems operate: that success is determined by effort or ability rather than by class background. (Sowinska 1993, 151–2).

For this minority group as well as the others, life within the walls of the ivory tower proves far less empowering than the institution promised during its recruiting efforts.

REALITIES

"Where the traits of Otherness converge," says Quinnan, "the perceptible level of opposition is certain to intensify" (30). Opposition to the Other being seen or heard on campus; sharing fairly in resources distributed among students; being treated with respect and having their work treated with respect as well—and every minority characteristic—multiplies the quantity of opposition to a student's existence. Women are treated unfairly, and women of color more unfairly than white women. Students of color are treated unfairly, and gay students of color even more so. Working-class gays, older women, older working-class gays . . . the potential for discrimination goes on and on and on. The university cannot and does not hide its hypocrisy:

> No matter how progressive the curriculum or empowering the pedagogy, at most colleges institutional decision making is hierarchical, resource allocation is competitive, and differences are conceptualized and treated as sources of conflict. (Guarasci & Cornwell 1997, 160)

Even if faculty don't notice the irony inherent in the contrast their claim to support democratic goals and their blatant discrimination against the Other, say Guarasci and Cornwell, students certainly will. No wonder so many leave, especially so many from non-dominant groups. Until universities stop marginalizing so many students in so many ways, they have no right to claim to be democratic, egalitarian institutions.

CHAPTER 5
Power and the Dissertation
Faculty as Demigods

> *I will spare the reader further recounting of the inanities (and horrors) of the Ph.D.—the oral "qualifying exam," the rejected dissertation, the lost dissertation, the delayed dissertation. It is all too grim for words. In any event, that the Ph.D. is an incubus on higher education can, I assume, hardly be doubted.*
> —PAGE SMITH

RITUAL AND GATEKEEPING

Tradition and ritual are elemental in academe, where the highest ranked institutions still inscribe their diplomas in Latin—so that a holder of an *A.B.* from an ivied institution will firmly correct anyone who mistakenly refers to it as a *B.A.* (never mind that both designations refer to the same degree level). Faculty still don traditional robes and gold-tasseled headgear for such occasions as commencement, parading like peacocks in the colors that signify their *alma mater*s, their specific degrees, their specific areas of expertise. Leading such academic parades are officers of the institution, and often the vice provost or someone similar bears a ceremonial mace, the time-honored symbol of the institutional power wielded by faculty and administrators, who award or deny degrees and shape the future of every student who comes to the institution seeking admission to the elevated company of those already robed in academic splendor.

There is no small irony in such a show serving as the culminating experience in higher education, especially in graduate education. The archaic academic dress, so impressive on ceremonial occasions, mirrors all too accurately universities' habit of maintaining any number of other, less benign academic traditions whose meaning has long since faded—like the meaning of the hoods and colors, always meticulously explained in commencement programs for the benefit of the uninitiated. Tenaciously, universities cling to rituals as irrelevant in modern meaningful education as the ceremonial mace is in modern warfare. And yet, as the ceremonial mace might serve well enough to club an unarmed foe to death, some of the last ritualistic hurdles a graduate student must surmount can be made equally deadly. Chief among these—as indicated by the fact that one in every four students who reach ABD status never finishes a doctorate—is the dreaded dissertation, the last hurdle before joining the godly ranks of the Ph.D. (Bowen & Rudenstine 1992, 253).

> The "dissertation experience" has been ingrained in American higher education as the crowning achievement of those who desire a Ph.D. since the first Ph.D. was granted by Yale in 1861. Moore (1985) describes this final hurdle: "Of all the sacred cows of academia, the Ph.D. dissertation is the most holy. The idea that to attain academia's crown jewel you must make an original contribution to knowledge in your field is an unquestionable item of faith. That the dissertation process should be a long, ego threatening, gut wrenching experience goes without saying. That a dissertation is not acceptable until a committee of professors who could not agree on the time of day, all agree to accept your complex work is academia's most unshakable rubric" (127). Excellence, then, so far as Ph.D. attainment is concerned, means completion of a dissertation. (Hanson 1992, 5)

No matter how sacred the dissertation may seem, however, its usefulness is questionable—at best. Perhaps one of the most disturbing features of the dissertation requirement is that even when it was first instituted, it was an exercise designed more to manage students than to provide a meaningful educational experience. In arguing for a different kind of experience, Damrosch (1995) includes a quotation from Ira Remsen, a member of one of Johns Hopkins' early graduate programs, who has explained the dissertation's original function largely as a control mechanism:

> "At first, we thought it would be sufficient simply to let the students come together and select their courses . . . [but] there was a good deal of indefinite browsing. They would fly from one thing to another. . . . And those of us who were charged with the management of affairs concluded that we must take advantage of the degree. We must offer something to keep these students in line. The Ph.D. degree was the next thing after the A.B. degree, and we recognized that we must offer this in order to keep that body of workers in line, and that, in order to secure the results we wanted, it was also necessary to require a piece of

research as a requisite for that degree. That is the machinery we used. We thought at first, that we might avoid it, but found that we must adopt it." (33)

However indispensable the dissertation in its current form might seem today, it was not a self-evident academic requirement when it was instituted. On the contrary, even in its infancy its function was largely to assure faculty of control over students.

Instead of evolving into a productive scholarly experience, the dissertation has continued to function primarily as a gatekeeping device, so that it now appears to be one of Wilshire's university "purification rituals . . . notoriously deep and pervasive archaic practices [which are] still at work in the obscured background" (1990, 162). In this sense, the dissertation functions as a trial by fire that purifies and hardens the worthy (those who manage to survive) and eliminates the unworthy masses (those who can still be driven out at this point). Openly functioning as a weeding mechanism, the dissertation requirement demonstrates the university's tenacity in clinging to outmoded practice and its refusal to consider the best interests of its students rather than its own needs:

> The [university can] change constantly at the local level while varying little in many basic ways, so that contemporary concerns can coexist with very archaic procedures and values. Sedimented levels of history overlay one another, punctuated by igneous extrusions from the deep past. One of the world's chief centers of high-tech research, the American university, is also in many ways a holdover from the Middle Ages, complete with an entrenched guild mentality and the indentured servitude of graduate student apprentices and postdoctoral journeymen. (Damrosch 1995, 18)

While the university may consider itself modern and responsive to changing times with banks of blinking computer screens glowing in state-of-the-art labs, classrooms, lecture halls, and even dormitories, many of its practices—the dissertation for one—remain unexamined and do not serve the needs of today's students.

Today's ritual dissertation is so educationally bankrupt, in fact, that it cannot even pretend to constitute real world practice in research and writing. Baird (1996), even though he is not among those overtly challenging the practice, says that he himself tells students "that a dissertation is like no other writing they have done before or will do again" (29).

If the dissertation format is strictly an academic idiosyncrasy—like the five paragraph essay format which is so often foisted upon undergraduates despite the fact that it is a format found nowhere else—how can it prepare a scholar for his or her life's work? In fact, in an article highly critical of current practices, Ziolkowski (1990) notes the difference between what is often called "dissertation-ese" and effective research and writing:

> Many a new Ph.D. revising a dissertation for publication has discovered that the first things that must go are the introductory survey of research, the lengthy footnotes, and the cumbersome bibliographical apparatus often required for the dissertation. It would be far more helpful to the student's career as a scholar to learn the style used most widely in journals of the field, to practice the art of selective quotation, and to recite the credo of scholarly ethics. (194)

As critical as Ziolkowski's comments are, they seem almost gentle compared to Smith's characterization of dissertations and "dissertationese":

> It was as a candidate for the Ph.D. at Harvard that I first encountered the Cult of Dullness. Since boyhood I had aspired to be a writer. I was not sure what kind of a writer, but some kind. So with my first graduate research paper I tried to write as well as I could. My professor, the urbane Crand Brinton, warned me gently that, although he himself did not object to a well-written paper (I don't see how it could have been *very* well written at best; it was on some obscure point of natural law), his colleagues might be put off. They might suspect that I was not really committed to dull writing (he didn't put it exactly that way) and thus not a suitable candidate for the Ph.D. I encountered the problem again when I sent my doctoral dissertation to a typist to have it typed up for presentation to my readers, who would approve or disapprove it. The typist called shortly to express her concern. It did not read like a Ph.D. Was I sure it would be acceptable? What was the problem? I asked. Well, she was enjoying reading it, and that made her uneasy on my account. She was concerned that it might not be accepted. It was not as dull as she felt it ought to be. . . . The Cult of Dullness not only survives; it flourishes. (1990, 110–111)

Dull. Obscure. Impractical. Smith continues his characterization of the dissertation:

> Not only is the Ph.D. dissertation constrained by the requirement that it be original (in the sense of dealing with material never dealt with before) and dull; it must also conform to the prejudices of the examiners. In other words, it must not be too original. Especially on the theoretical side, it must be compatible with the current "thinking" in the field. It must not be too advanced, and it must have no truck with notions now considered obsolete (although in fact these obsolete notions often return in time as the latest finding). It thus manages the not inconsiderable feat of being both stultifying and capricious. (112)

Yet the dissertation—born largely of a need to keep students in line, used more as a hazing ritual to screen out the unsuitable than as a meaningful educational experience, and offering the student little of use in a life after graduate school—survives, even thrives, and is trumpeted and feared as the final test of who will ultimately prove worthy.

The cost to students is incalculable, if routinely ignored by most in the academy:

> From our perspective, the disturbing findings for both attrition and the amount of time invested are associated with later stages of graduate study. Post-first year attrition has drifted upward, as has the time spent in achieving ABD status (Table 13.1). The percentage of students who never earn PhDs, in spite of having achieved ABD status, has risen in both larger and smaller programs, as has the time spent at the dissertation stage by those who completed doctorates. The direction of change is unmistakable, and the absolute numbers are high enough to be grounds for serious concern. (Bowen & Rudenstine, 253)

Students are spending more and more time in doctoral programs and writing dissertations, and yet fewer and fewer survive. Effective quality control or reified oppression of students? A close look at students' lived experience of the dissertation process answers that it must be judged oppressive, a means for faculty to use and maintain their hegemonic privileges for their own, rather than students', benefit.

DILEMMAS AND DEMIGODS

Every aspect of the dissertation enterprise presents to students a new set of power struggles and a wide variety of opportunities to fail, opportunities that often have nothing to do with their own abilities. First, a student must find a topic limited enough to be manageable and yet sophisticated enough to be deemed worthy of serving as a topic for the near-mythical dissertation—while also being sufficiently interesting to the student to make several years' work on it endurable. This challenge is followed by that of finding an advisor who can and will sponsor a dissertation on that particular topic, using a methodology that interests the student. And if the student can find an advisor who is also humane, predictable, and accessible, so much the better. Then, the student must assemble a full and effective committee, no small challenge in a world of competing egos and turf lords. Finally, the student must manage to survive the dissertation defense, where potentially damning, quarrelsome issues often relate not to the quality of the student's work but to the professorial habit of opposing, on principle, *anything* which another faculty member, especially from a competing discipline, department or paradigm, supports.

Committing to a Topic

Bowen and Rudenstine (1992) find that for all students, and especially for students in English, history, and political science (EHP), the struggle to identify a workable topic often proves the most difficult stage of work on the dissertation, one during which students are particularly vulnerable.

> By virtually all accounts, the time between the end of course work and the moment of energetic engagement with a dissertation topic is an unusually vulnerable time for many graduate students in the EHP fields. Selection of a topic appears to have become an increasingly formidable task, at a time when the expectations of many faculty (and institutions) concerning the dissertation have become more demanding than ever. . . .
>
> [A difficulty] mentioned more often than any other hurdle is selecting an appropriate topic for a doctoral dissertation. It is not uncommon for students to spend between one and two years searching for the "right" topic and preparing a dissertation prospectus. (14, 254)

Why such difficulty simply to identify a topic? Often, the answer to that question lies in one or both of two primary areas: the rhetoric about what a dissertation must be and the need for the topic to be acceptable to key players.

A graduate student is told that the dissertation topic is the foundation for a substantive piece of original research, one that must make a significant contribution to new knowledge in the field. Given that it is a commonplace in academe that much "research" published in contemporary journals falls far short of this goal, how realistic can it be for novice researchers to meet it in their first research effort? Still, graduate students, unless they had the good luck to learn from some good-natured source about the gap between rhetoric and reality, begin their research weighed down by the burden of finding a topic that will yield some significant new piece of information in a specific field. In her student advocate/advisor stance, Hawley outlines this dilemma and warns students about devoting themselves to an impossible cause (1993):

> Unfortunately, thousands of students have been burdened with the idea that nothing short of a *magnum opus* will do. They waste months and years trying to achieve the impossible, or at least the impractical. Now is not the ideal time, nor is the dissertation the ideal vehicle, to produce a deathless *tome*. Realize at the outset that your dissertation is unlikely to make your name a household word or to shake the foundations of your discipline. View it as an exercise in scholarship that will make a modest contribution to the body of knowledge and be an asset in your search for a faculty position. (32)

While Hawley is quite right about the likely futility and certain delay born of searching for *the* right topic, even students who have been given such advice may not be able to act on it and set more modest goals for a possible topic. After all, as established in Chapter Two, all institutions and institutional representatives must care deeply about their reputations—and the more impossible a program is to complete, the more favorably (if perversely so) it tends to be regarded by outsiders. As Ziolkowski (1990) notes,

> Here matters have changed little since the days of William James, who noted that among his colleagues "two antagonistic passions, one for multiplying as much as possible the annual output of doctors, the other for raising the standard of difficulty in passing, so that the Ph.D. of the special institution shall carry a higher blaze of distinction than it does elsewhere." These antagonistic passions manifest themselves today in pressures with which every graduate dean is familiar: to increase the number of graduate students in every department while, at the same time, extending the expectations (and the time) for the degree. (189–190)

Not surprisingly, the quest for making requirements more and more difficult has led, among other things, to longer dissertations (the very *tomes* Hawley notes are not feasible at the point of dissertation) and increased time-to-degree.

> It is not without significance that time-to-degree almost precisely parallels the average length of dissertations by field. From 1920 to the present, total time-to-degree has consistently ranged from a low point in the physical sciences by way of engineering and the life sciences to the social sciences and professional fields, with its peak in the humanities. According to the survey upon which Bernard Berelson based his study, the length of dissertations accepted in 1957–58 (by the median number of pages) extended from the physical sciences (105 pages) and life sciences (108 pages), by way of engineering (136 pages) and the professional fields (171 pages), to the social sciences (236 pages) and the humanities (285 pages). There are of course many local variations. . . .
>
> Bulk has not always been a prerequisite in humanities dissertations. When James Morris Whiton qualified for one of the first three Yale Ph.D.'s in 1861, he submitted a six-page handwritten thesis in Latin on the proverb *Brevis vita, ars longa*. . . . By 1968, Don Cameron Allen, in a study on the Ph.D. in English and American literature, estimated that 53 percent of the dissertations in the field came to between 151 and 300 pages, another 32 percent ranged from 301 to 500 pages, and 6 percent amounted to 500 pages or more. (Ziolkowski 1990, 190–91)

To determine a topic, then, the student must first either be disabused of the idea that an excessively lengthy and cumbersome work is necessary and/or must find an advisor who actually endorses that idea, contrary to institutional rhetoric and despite concerns about institutional reputation. The latter is a chicken-and-egg problem, however, since one's dissertation advisor might most usefully be someone well versed in the area one chooses to research—which the student may not be able to identify without a helpful advisor.

But even students fortunate enough to begin with a clear idea of their research interests and an eagerness to work in certain fields are not spared problems in settling on a topic and composing a prospectus. As discussed in Chapter Four, universities have many unspoken norms and many conceptions of what constitutes Other. Not surprisingly, the Other often has particular difficulty finding approval for research topics, which most often center on issues central to their Otherness. Feminists, for example, may well have difficulty in a heavily male and empiricist institution finding a sponsor for a feminist and constructivist dissertation. For gay and lesbian students, the problem of identifying an acceptable topic is particularly intense—even if a sponsor for a dissertation on gay issues can be found, the topic can still cause the student a great deal of grief. For example, one student reports that even after finding a sponsor, she was warned away from gay topics by other faculty, harassed by professors who didn't approve of her research, and eventually jeopardized by a vice chancellor who could not accept her research topic:

> The vice chancellor who had given me some $800 toward my research for the thesis took me aside one day and told me "I supported your research financially, but I want you to know, I never supported the topic." I thanked him for adding to my qualitative data for my thesis on "attitudes undergraduates have toward gay men and lesbians" and said I would put his comments into the campus climate description. However, I was not permitted to add his comments, and I was told "Don't bite the hand that feeds you." The v.c. himself even told me later that he had considered not letting me back into the program the next year. I doubt he could have done that, but it was clear he really didn't like me. I went through hell that summer. I actually thought about quitting, but my research was too important to me. The most support I got from anyone was over the internet from a colleague. . . . The struggles had an enormous impact on me. I lost a lot of weight, I started drinking heavily that summer and I wanted to commit suicide. I checked myself into a VA treatment center and stayed there for a month. I had to get away and that was better than killing myself. In retrospect, that was the worst experience of my life. I firmly believe that if I were writing/researching "first year college students' experiences" or some such topic, I would never have encountered any problems—and of course—if I were closeted, everyone would have been more comfortable and happy. (l.)

Even after a successful defense, the decision to commit to a topic that the mainstream deems "unacceptable" can haunt a student:

> Just after my defense I was told that my dissertation title would not be published in the commencement program, a violation of the university's tradition. The title, I was told, was too offensive

> [since it mentioned the silence of lesbian and gay teachers] and some attendees might not like it. . . . I had to threaten them with a lawsuit which they must have decided would bring far more attention to the publication, so they published the title with absolutely no subsequent fallout. . . . My dissertation to this day is still not in their library—but my book will be in bookstores in October! (O.)

Selecting and committing to a dissertation topic, then, is no small task—not only because dissertations are characterized by the same sort of grandiose rhetoric used in admissions materials, but also because the student's future (not to mention mental and physical health) can be dramatically affected by his or her choice.

Faculty Advisors

To navigate the dangers of doctoral programs—and most especially its dissertation phase—the support of faculty is critical to students. The nature of the relationship between advisor and advisee is particularly important:

> Several studies showed that both male and female students' satisfaction with doctoral programs, particularly with the dissertation, was directly related to satisfaction with advisement relationships [4, 7, 10]. If, as this research indicated, the advisor-advisee relationship was the single most important element in graduate education, why was it so often perceived as the most disappointing relationship in many doctoral students' experiences [5, 7]? (Heinrich 1991, 515)

Like other elements of graduate study—and as in other situations where one group is fully empowered over another—too often there is a chasm between the ideal and the real.

Ideally, the advisor functions as mentor:

> Mentors, in contrast to advisors, do more than simply stand and point the way. Mentors accompany their protégés throughout the entire process. This calls for a professional and emotional investment of a different order, one characterized by a strong commitment to the student as a person as well as a neophyte scholar. . . . [A] similar benevolent figure appears in the *Divine Comedy* when Virgil materializes at

critical times during Dante's long and hazardous passage through the bizarre and dangerous nether regions in search of Beatrice. Virgil is the perfect mentor; knowledgeable, trustworthy, and caring. Moreover, he is a seasoned traveler, having trod that path many times before, and he interprets enigmatic signs, warns of dangers ahead, and steadies the faltering steps of his protégé. On the other hand, he is clearly no patsy. He forces Dante to develop his own resources by using just the right mix of challenge, inspiration, discipline, and support. (Hawley 1993, 52–3)

A mentor is a sort of trail guide, warning students of assorted dangers, pointing out the challenges that can be surmounted and lead to growth, cheerleading good efforts, outlawing self-defeating mediocrity and laziness, and providing faith to fuel a student's progress.

Unfortunately, many sources report that mentors are exceedingly rare. Hawley (1993), in a section referring to mentors as "rare individuals," notes that "It is an exceptional dissertation chair who deserves to be called a *mentor*" (51). Heinrich's study of advising/mentoring of women students yielded findings common in all studies of mentoring—that such relationships are both exceedingly important and exceedingly rare:

This study supports the mentoring literature in these findings: (1) mentoring relationships were rare and precious—only eight of the fifty-two male advisors represented in this sample were called mentors; (2) women who had mentoring advisement relationships felt professionally affirmed and were more productive after graduation; and (3) because both male and female advisors were called mentors, advisory behavior, not gender, distinguished mentoring from nonmentoring advisors [3, 7]. (Heinrich 1991, 519)

Given the evidence that mentoring is critical to perseverance, satisfaction, and success, why do so few relationships develop?

First, as Hawley (1993) notes, such relationships cannot be institutionally mandated since at least in part they "emerge somewhat mysteriously out of the chemistry between two people and out of a shared interest in the discipline" (51). In this sense, mentoring can no more be imposed upon two people than genuine friendship can be; the pair is a good fit personally, or it is not.

However, the reward system of the institution and the unchecked power of faculty work to undermine a climate that would routinely foster such relationships. While good relationships cannot be mandated, they certainly can be encouraged or discouraged—and the latter is too often the case.

For example, students are aware that having a "big name" supervise a dissertation is an asset in the academic job market where, as noted in earlier chapters, reputation functions as institutional capital. Unfortunately, what the institution expects from "names" is not good mentoring, but increased research productivity, which again enhances both "the name's" career and the institution's reputation. Therefore, there is most often no institutional interest, and certainly no reward, encouraging a "big name" professor to develop good relationships with graduate students:

> The advantages of working with giants notwithstanding, some BIG NAMES can be inordinately preoccupied with their own research and publications, speaking engagements, consultancies, campus politics, and the like. Full professors who have arrived, academically speaking, may be singularly disinterested in sponsoring a novice unless this person shows unusual promise as a research assistant or as a potential "disciple" who can make substantive contributions to the BIG NAME's own work. More than one doctoral candidate has discovered the typical *modus operandi*, that the student does all the work and the sponsor gets all of the credit. (Hawley 1993, 55)

Since the institution and professor both benefit from such exploitation, and only the student loses, little has been done to protect students from such abuse and its resulting bitterness.

On the other hand, other dangers come with selecting a junior faculty member as advisor, as one student reports:

> She was busy establishing her own career, research agenda, and whatever, so months could pass without my receiving responses to email and phone calls. (U.)

Needless to say, an advisor who is too busy for graduate students and inaccessible to them is not only of no help, but an additional hindrance.

Problems with access and communication are ubiquitous, certainly in part because few, if any, institutions have established clear expectations for relationships between advisors and students, even at a minimal level. The lack of expectation is not surprising, given that one of the privileges of faculty is near total freedom in how they execute their responsibilities.

As a result, the nature of an advising relationship is most often defined solely by the faculty member because after all, the faculty member is the one holding institutional power in such relationships. The student, then, is utterly dependent on the faculty member's sense of what should be appropriate, too often formulated without any particular attention to an individual student's unique needs. Such idiosyncrasy is an environmental hazard for students, as Bowen and Rudenstine document (1992):

> Interviews with faculty members at a number of the universities participating in this study revealed a wide range of attitudes and practices. At one extreme, some faculty are just "too busy" and give advising low priority. At the other extreme, many faculty seem to take it for granted that if they agree to act as a dissertation adviser, they will hold regular meetings with the student, set up a schedule, make certain from the beginning that the topic is feasible and researchable, request outlines and chapters at specific moments, and "see the student through." More common, however, was the attitude—unquestionably genuine—that "my door is always open," or "students who wish to see me can always count on the fact that I will make myself available." This approach works well with certain students, but it is obviously insufficient for the person who is uncertain, who feels unable or unwilling to confront an adviser before feeling "in control" of all the relevant materials, or who may even call once or twice and purely by chance not find the adviser available just at that moment.
>   In these cases, students do in fact often drift without guidance for considerable periods of time, while faculty members continue to operate on the presumption that their declared accessibility and their genuine interest in students, are sufficient to make the process work. If a student fails to appear for weeks, or perhaps months, there may be no "call" sent out, no direct assertion of control undertaken by the faculty member. Meanwhile, the student may be lost in bibliographic or other thickets, and is almost bound to think that he or she cannot have a conversation with the adviser because such an encounter will only reveal deep areas of ignorance or vulnerability. Months go by, the psychological barriers grow greater (on the student's part), and the adviser's door remains open but undarkened by the candidate's presence. (260)

In cases like the latter, the faculty member—who in fact has institutional control of the situation—simply uses the privilege to foist responsibility upon students, who may or may not assume the power and responsibility they have suddenly been given. On second thought, what power has the student been given? Actually, none. The illusory transfer of power to the student is insidious since the faculty member retains the power to accept or dismiss any of the student's work and is therefore still in control. It's a no-lose situation for the faculty member, and a difficult one for many students who, hesitating to reveal to their advisors all that they do not know, are loathe to ask for help. In an environment where there are no ground rules for behavior, and for a student with no prior experience in approaching dissertations, such sudden freedom can be deadly.

Again, however, escaping this dilemma doesn't ensure student safety. Even when advisors are perfectly specific about their expectations regarding interactions, students can still be endangered, as this student reports:

> My story could start with a third committee chair, my first having left the institution—fortunately for me because I learned he rarely proceeded in a timely manner to get his students through a program. I also had trouble getting responses from him. One time he told me he'd take a draft of my proposal on a trip and call me upon his return. I allowed a reasonable amount of time to pass before "bugging" him, only to be told HE was having trouble dealing with my lack of communication with him! I did remind him of what he had said; and because it was via email, I had it documented. Naturally, he didn't apologize. (Z.)

Why would he apologize? The absolute power of faculty over students means that they can simply respond to students who complain as Walt Whitman answered his critics in *Leaves of Grass:* "Do I contradict myself? Very well then, I contradict myself." Who can override poetic—or professorial—license?

Given such license, it is not surprising that dysfunctional relationships between students and advisors are much more commonly identified than mentoring relationships. Of three archetypal types of relationships Heinrich (1995) identified between female students and advisors, for example, only one—which she refers to as a "power with" relationship—assumes the characteristics of a mentoring relationship, involving "collegial sharing of power" (450). In each of the other types, power was misused by the advisor. The advisor either created a "power over" relationship in which advisees were expected to "be self-motivated and to accomplish without the need for advisory emotional support" or a "power disowned" relationship in which advisees needed to become "overadequate" in order to compensate for the influence of a negative or inadequate advisor (453).

Hawley, too, identifies a variety of advising roles that can be problematic for students. Though noting that her characterizations are "typecast and deliberately exaggerated," she also notes that there is enough truth in each description for the student to be wary of the type (1993, 58). She includes in her list of "Professors to Avoid": the autocrat, who "insists upon dictating [the student's] every move"; the judge/jury, who gives the student "no help at all, just says aye or nay about everything . . . like a Roman emperor"; the opportunist, who treats the student as "an academic slave to promote her own career," and the worst of whom will "usurp [the student's] best ideas and fail to credit . . . contributions, knowing there isn't much [a student] can do about it"; the sexist, who is especially difficult because "the perpetrator can always feign innocence, claiming the victim is unduly sensitive to 'women's issues'"; and the seducer/seductress, "arguably the most dangerous—to [a student's] professional goals and . . . personal and emotional well-being" (58–59). In each of these cases, it is the student who pays the price for the faculty member's power abuse. Students must fully yield autonomy, try to beg help from others, suffer exploitation silently, educate the faculty member about gender issues, try to avoid unwanted advances or to maintain an academic relationship with the complications of a romantic one. Or they could simply go through the messy process of trying to replace one advisor with another—always politically dangerous.

Such analyses are rare, however, and most graduate students begin the process of developing a relationship with an advisor innocent of the dangers. As Sork, Chapman, and Butterwick note (1999):

> While the student-supervisor relationship is at the heart of the graduate education experience, it is rarely used as a site for the analysis of what Tisdell (1993) has called "interlocking systems of power, privilege and oppression in adult higher education."

Because the relationship is so often unexamined, a faculty member need not be callously exploitive or uncaring for problem relationships to arise, as Baird notes (1996):

> Even when the relationship is proceeding well, issues about the degree of appropriate involvement, dependency, and sometimes unconscious manipulation are present. (30)

The challenge of simply identifying and working with an advisor, then, is a formidable one for students.

Dissertation Committees and Defenses

The challenges of identifying an advisor are multiplied when the student attempts to put together a committee, the body that will eventually decide whether the dissertation is acceptable—and whether the degree will or will not be awarded. While all faculty members have power over students, they also have unequal amounts of power among themselves, a situation that can cause a variety of problems for students. A student may find, for example, that the chair has less power than another committee member, so that the advice the chair gives and the student must follow can be contradicted and undermined by another member, as in this case reported by Heinrich (1991):

> One woman's third committee member left just as she finished coursework. Her remaining committee was composed of an inadequate major advisor and his department head. She recounted: "It was apparent to me that my advisor was not controlling the committee. The second person was controlling it because he was the department chair. So my advisor didn't have the power to argue with him...." She went to the Dean of the college, explained the situation, and requested him to become the third advisor to restabilize the power balance. He agreed and his presence re-empowered her major advisor by outranking the major advisor's department chair. (527)

This student was uncommonly fortunate in being able to right the power balance, but first she had to accurately identify the problem and be able to identify and work out the solution, an addition to the already formidable task of composing the dissertation.

Besides power inequalities, there are any number of other complications committee members can bring into the dissertation defense that—though they have no bearing on the student's work—strongly affect judgments relevant to the dissertation under consideration. For example, disciplinary conflicts can affect the progress of committee thinking. If he or she is very lucky, the student may emerge from such a power struggle simply sadder but wiser:

> My advisor had a half position in each of two departments, and during a college reorganization (from botany and zoology to or-

> ganismal, molecular and ecology, more or less) the members of my doctoral committee were at odds with each other. One very aged and highly respected physiologist got his feelings hurt, and it took a lot of stroking to get things moving again. I felt caught up, and fortunately got the reputation for being able to deal with "difficult" people. It didn't come back to haunt me, but I certainly learned a lot about the politics of academia. It made me extremely gun-shy about campus politics. (R.)

Sometimes the political struggles among faculty members are much more significant, however, and the cost to the student much greater, as in this case:

> The defense became what I felt was a mob scene. (My advisor later confided to me that he had never seen a "more cantankerous committee.") Tables and discussion that had been removed from earlier drafts were requested; the implications were considered too broad (something my advisor and I still feel is "wrong" but we're not fighting it). The basis of developmental theory—one of my important considerations—was "trashed" because (essentially) if there is no research to prove that humans can learn/improve the trait I was studying, the idea of human development as continuing growth and change cannot be included in any shape or form.
>
> I was informed by the committee that I had passed the defense, done a good piece of research, but in NO WAY could I make revisions and get them thru the committee in the 3 weeks left.... I had left the meeting feeling as tho' I had somehow failed anyway; whatever victory there was, was indeed hollow. Since it was close to Easter, the image of a chocolate bunny filled my head. I had expected to bite into a solid bunny and found only a shell. On the 2½ hour ride home, I began to feel more and more like that bunny, or the reverse of The Velveteen Rabbit—no longer alive, but stuffed—only my stuffing had been knocked from me. How could I explain to friends and family that the defense was successful, but I still wouldn't make the long-anticipated May graduation? ...
>
> Commentary on [my revised] draft came almost 2 weeks after I had submitted it. I made the newly suggested changes, and along the way, found committee members who didn't remember at all what my dissertation was about or even what they

had suggested I do to improve it. Help that was promised at the defense was not provided, but I muddled through and submitted another "final" draft. Naturally, my advisor was off presenting something somewhere, but he had been back more than a week before I received a phone call or email. I felt like a teenager waiting for that "special someone" to call and ask me for a date. Before he left town, my advisor agreed that I should be able to have this wrapped up by the end of May, but that didn't happen. One committee member was away for two weeks, missing my advisor's request that members comment on the revised dissertation by June 1. Before that person returned, everyone else had signed off, but my advisor felt he should give him "as long as it takes" to respond, adding that he didn't anticipate any problems. I reminded my advisor that he'd be leaving June 10 and I'd like to have this settled. (W.)

Deadlines for student graduation seem to mean little to faculty members; comments that cause students weeks of additional work are made so offhandedly that, in a very short time, the faculty members themselves have no idea what they said. Here, perhaps, is the ultimate powerlessness a student can experience: years of study and work invested in a project that will be accepted or not based partly on a constellation of personalities who happen to be in this or that position or mood when they come together to configure a defense committee on a given day.

The consequences can even extend far beyond the extra weeks or months of work imposed on a student. One student's advisor, among the most powerful on her institution's faculty, unexpectedly set a hostile tone at the defense of her student. The advisor objected not to the quality of the research but to the pedagogy used in the classroom providing data for the dissertation. Because the dissertation topic was wholly unrelated to teaching methodology, criticism of it was irrelevant to the dissertation—but that didn't stop the advisor from attacking it. Since the other members of the committee were far junior to the advisor, they remained silent, although one later returned a copy of the dissertation to its writer, with praise for the work noted on nearly every page.

Betrayed without warning by the person on whom she most depended and with no other member willing to say a single word on her behalf, the dissertation writer felt herself to be an utter failure even though she technically passed the defense. Because of the hostility of the meeting and the extraordinary revisions required, she left the meeting feeling that her doctorate would be a fake, something she'd ultimately been given out of charity rather than something she'd earned with a solid piece of research and writing. The effect was both devastating and lifelong:

> I have never been so devastated in my whole life—not by my father's death, not by anything—as I was by my dissertation defense. I don't think that I will ever completely recover from it.

While these cases may sound extreme to some readers, the reality is that such deeply personal and negative consequences are far from rare. Even Jane Tompkins, an extraordinary successful academic whose career has been spent at some of the country's most prestigious institutions, has spoken openly about the psychic cost of her doctorate (1996):

> In order to shoulder the enormous workload graduate school imposed, I couldn't let myself know a fraction of what was going on inside. It was only years later that I discovered how much I had hated Yale. On my first trip to New Haven my stomach went into a knot as my foot touched the pavement; during the entire visit I was filled with anger, disappointment, frustration, outrage, and despair, as if the feelings had remained in the air above New Haven, waiting to alight on my head the day I showed up again. (77)

The price students pay for faculty abuse of power within the academy is only partly indicated by statistics on attrition and the number of ABDs. Even those who succeed often pay far more dearly than outsiders suspect, sometimes with installments of bitterness, cynicism, and a sense of failure and/or unworthiness stretching out over their lifetimes. This price is indefensible.

CHAPTER 6
Voices of the Oppressed[1]

> *If this all sounds farfetched, try something. The next time you get the opportunity to talk to someone who has run the Ph.D. gauntlet, or even better, someone who started but dropped out, ask him about his experience. Did he find it fair, challenging? Did he think he was treated well, with respect? There is no better way to understand what is involved than to listen to the pain and anguish of one who has experienced it.*
> —MARTIN ANDERSON

In the end, the most compelling evidence that graduate education needs serious reform is found in the lived experience of students. For that reason, this chapter offers a place where students speak for themselves, in their own voices, and without the interference of editorial comment. For the thoughtful reader, this chapter also offers brief glimpses of how things might be otherwise, a topic fully explored in the final chapter that follows.

CHRIS

One thing I remember about when I first started: I felt like a fish out of water. I don't know why I didn't think about it before I applied, but this is an extremely rural white town and I'm from an extremely urban Black town. That was very, very hard to deal with at first. I just wasn't used to being around that many White people and being the only Black person. That was the first time I would walk on a street and not see another Black person, Hispanic person, or for that matter another Asian person. It bothered me. It really, really bothered me.

---

[1] All narratives in this chapter have been culled from taped interviews with volunteers. The transcripts have been edited to make the written narratives easier to read and more coherent. The words, thoughts, and stories, however, come entirely from the speakers.

I remember the first time it dawned on me. It was the first day of class. I had gotten on the bus to travel in and I remember—I will never forget how I felt. It was a sea of white. That was the first thing in my mind. I said "Oh my God, this is like walking into a sea of white." I had never seen so many White people before in my life all together at one time. I'm used to cities, where when you walk down the street you see a little bit of everybody. New York, or someplace like that. I was not prepared to see all White people.

And along with that, I didn't think the people were friendly at all. It would be nothing for me to walk down the street and no one would speak to me. It would be like I was invisible walking around the campus—and that was White people and that was even some Black people too. I remember thinking "I can't believe this." I could definitely walk the whole of the campus without interacting with anybody—and anybody who's been on a big college campus knows that's a long time. In a mile and a half, I wouldn't get eye contact and, you know, even in New York City I can get eye contact with somebody. Maybe not speak to anyone, but somebody would at least look at me. On campus, I would just be invisible walking around. That was very, very bothersome.

Then, too, when I first got here, the minority coordinator told me that there was no money, that all the assistantships and scholarships, everything was given out. There was going to be no money for me at all. The best he could do was try to have me get a job, a regular 9 to 5 job with some tuition reduction. So I was devastated, of course. Because a professor who worked with me during my masters told me that he had got it all figured out. He said he would take care of it. In December, I asked him if I could send my stuff in early. He told me no. He said "Oh no, no, no. Don't do that." When I went in February, he didn't even know I was going. I found out he had never talked to anybody. He hadn't done anything. I was upset, but I talked to the lady in charge of fellowships and since I had such a high GPA in my Master's program, she was able to give me a fellowship for the next year. But she told me that she had no idea what the minority coordinator was talking about, because he had to submit everything to her and he hadn't turned in a list yet. That was the real kicker for me. He hadn't even turned in a list. So: he lied. And that bothered me doubly because he lied, number one, and number two, I'm thinking about the fact that there is supposed to be a minority representative helping us get here and if it had been up to him, I would never have been there at all.

My experience was a very lonely one, which was a shock to me because I just didn't expect that. I had always heard and assumed the grad students were together, like a little family, and they helped each other. I didn't find that at all. I found that everyone was very insular. Everyone was isolated. Now maybe that was my fault because I also had my son up there and I really didn't have time to go hang out at the happy hours and things like that when they offered it. But I felt like, there's got to be something else for people to do if they don't happen to like drinking at bars. I found out they're very much into that here. And I didn't think the adults had the same type of culture as the undergraduates: "Meet me at the bar." That's not really my thing. I just don't like doing that.

Some of this loneliness also came from the department I was in. When I first arrived I was in a different department, and that had a lot to do with it because that department was not together at all. They had just gotten a new person, and he is very egotistical—just not a good person. They tried to have little things to do; I remember they had a little pizza party. But it just didn't work out because there were so many things going wrong in the department, including that you couldn't get any classes. There were no professors. There were just about three professors. And when I took his classes, he was so arrogant he would piss you off so much during class it would be hard to go to a restaurant afterward and act like everything was okay.

Whenever we did go out socially, he was such a nice guy and it was a pleasure talking to him. But when he was in class he gave off the air "I know everything!" He was never interested in the kind of things that students wanted to discuss. Now I can't remember exactly, but I know I wanted to introduce something historically African American, something about *Plessy v. Ferguson*. I can remember that. And I could tell he was so totally disinterested. When I wrote a paper on it, he gave it back and talked about how it was okay but it was not on the graduate level. It needed a lot of work before it would be worthy of a Ph.D. And I was really like, "Damn." Because when I got my Master's, I had a 4.0. I had gotten all A's in that and I had written papers before and it really just shocked me. But I wasn't a baby about it. I didn't balk, I didn't bitch. I just basically said okay, fine. This is his opinion and we're all entitled to ours. But I didn't like it. And he was totally disinterested in what I wanted to do. When I wanted to leave the program and told him I was leaving, he didn't even say, "Oh, well, why are you leaving? What's going on? What's the problem? Why do you want to leave?" It was more like, "Oh, you're leaving? Okay. Write me a note to say that you're leaving and that you realize that you won't have your assistantship next year."

Another friend of mine and I both left the department about the same time. And we were the only two Black students in the department. The only Black professor, who is still in the department, asked me a while ago "Did anybody ever talk to you guys about you two being the only Black students in the department—and then leaving?" And I said no. The guy I'd had the problem with held so much weight because he was a new guy on the block; there were only about three of them in the department and he was the professor in charge. He was the anointed. And my thing was that I needed to get in and I needed to get out. I have my son. I had a life to get back to. I couldn't be up in grad school for four years lollygagging, going to every conference I could, taking all these wonderful great classes. And he told me, "Well, you know, it's not about getting out. It's about taking classes, grad school is." And I looked at him and said, "Everybody's experience doesn't have to be that." And he said again, "It's not about trying to get out." Immediately that told me he was not going to help me with my goal. He was not interested in what I needed to do. I needed somebody to be with who would talk to me and help me in my personal process, not tell me "Look, this is how we do it. Get with the program or get out."

I think he felt grad students were there to serve the faculty, because I remember that he made a comment about a grad assistant and said then that most grad students are grad assistants in some way, shape, or form. Very few of us just happen to understand that. He was talking about some work, and he said, "Well, I always give it to the grad assistants. You know, they're the slaves of the department." And the students all looked at him in shock, thinking, "Okay, tell me you didn't just say that." I mean, none of us could believe he just said that. First of all, that's an ignorant thing to say to group composed mostly of grad assistants. That was ignorant. And second, it was a rude thing to say because in that class were only two White and two Black Americans; the rest were from all other countries. I thought that was extremely insensitive to say because he doesn't know what kind of culture these people have been in. What if some of these cultures have involuntary servitude and some of the people here are trying to escape it? And here he's making light of it. I just didn't think that was funny. And I thought that was a very tacky thing to say. Here's the boss in charge, telling students straight out that there won't be any recourse if they feel they're getting some undue pressure from professors.

Actually, my major professor's my favorite person. He has so many students working with him, especially students of color, that I think it both hurts and it helps him. It helps [the university] because they know they need him to attract that contingent of students which looks good for them. So they were always very kind to me. They never had a nasty word to say about him to me, and they made sure I didn't want to leave the department. Any slight problem that I had was always solved. But I think that by the same token, it hurts him also because I've heard the comments other people in his department have made about him. I know the department head hates him, but he never showed that to me. He knew whose student I was. I think that you could definitely tell there was a power play going on there but I particularly tried to stay away from it. I made an effort not to get involved in any type of power plays or let myself get sucked into being on certain sides, because a student just can't win in those battles.

I ended up in one anyway, though, at my dissertation defense. There was a problem in the beginning because one of my professors decided to do a phone conference and I didn't know about that. The defense was on a Friday, and I didn't know he wasn't coming until Tuesday or Wednesday. He didn't even tell me. He told someone else who called someone else, whose wife called me. That wasn't too cool at all. Then, the graduate coordinator wasn't going to allow the phone conference and other members started calling me talking about how horrible the coordinator was. Finally I talked to him because I needed his signature and he explained his position, which made a lot of sense. He had a problem with the professor who wanted to phone in. He just didn't appreciate that, but he didn't say it directly to the professor. He did tell me, so I at least saw where he was coming from with it.

The problem was that the same guy had phone conferenced my comps. But the coordinator's thing was "He is not going to tell me that he didn't know about your defense weeks ago." Which he had, of course. At least a month before, he knew the date. The coordinator just didn't appreciate his coming up with this crap the week of the defense: "Oh, by the way. I'm not going to be there."

But I didn't even get the decency of him calling me and telling me he wasn't coming. He never e-mailed me. If it wasn't for a third party calling me, I wouldn't have known. And I needed to know because the defense was ungodly early, like 8:00 A.M., so I had to get the key and everything to have everybody come in. I had to get the instructions for the phone, make sure the phone was set up on time. I wouldn't have been able to handle all that if I had found out Thursday night. I didn't even get the decency of a phone call to say "I'm not going to be able to make it but I'm working it out so that I can get on the phone." Nothing. Nothing. Three days before the defense to find out a professor isn't coming and he's not getting approval from the grad school. And then he says, "Well you could switch the time." And I'm thinking, "Wait a minute here. You knew about this. I'm not switching anything. I'm sorry. Fly in. I'll put you up at a hotel if I have to but be there in the morning. I don't want to hear this." It was really a mess. I feel things like that happen to show you how you should not treat people.

I think that some people, once they finish they forget or they don't care anymore. I think a lot of it has to do with the mentality of "It happened to me and I dealt with it, so now you deal with it." There's no concern there for the grad students. Some people treat them like colleagues, but there are far too many of them who treat them like servants of the department or nobodies. They act as if you have no idea what you're talking about. But we're adults. And even undergrads deserve respect. People like to make the comment, "Well you're young." Being young doesn't mean being dumb and age doesn't mean wisdom. You see so clearly the power structure and how they're trying to use you. I always felt like I was being used for ulterior motives. I know one woman wanted to be on my committee because she was up for tenure review. So she needed something to look good and so she also asked me one time if she could be my co-chair because she was going up for review. At the time, you don't care. You're a student, you don't care. You just want to get this thing over with. But it's those kinds of experiences that play on your mind because you have to deal with so many people and so many different ways and it's like they don't care.

I found there's so many professors who feel like you're working for them, they're not working for you, straight up. This is an institution for their purposes. This is not an institution for learning; it's an institution for them to do research. You're a mere cog in the whole scheme of things. That's how I feel: some professors see grad students just really like a hindrance to their work. Or they just use them in doing their own studies and doing their own projects and don't even give students a chance to do their own work. One young female professor shocked me because when I had her she seemed wonderful, but they say she worked her grad assistant so hard she never even got her comps done and now she's left. That student has left. She's nowhere. She can't even leave and be ABD.

That's a problem because, I'm sorry, no matter what anybody thinks, I'm not here for you. I didn't come to grad school to be your assistant. If that's the case I'd be an administrative assistant or a researcher or whatever that title is called. But I'm not here for you. I'm here to get my work done. But I also say that that is that person's downfall because she should have said that. I mean my thing was my own education was a priority above all else. I wasn't there to do everybody else's work. Luckily I never did a grad assistantship with any of the professors. We're all adults and you have to stick up for yourself. If you allow yourself to be used, people will use you. And sometimes that hurts, to know that people will go ahead and take advantage of someone's kindness because that person doesn't know how to say no, but that's the truth and you have to tell them "I'm sorry, but I've worked my hours and now I have to go home, and I have to write for myself." But if you don't say it, they darn sure aren't going to say it for you.

I remember telling this professor, he was not in my department, how I was finished with my classes and I was just going to read through my comps or something like that, and he told me "Well, that's mighty fast, isn't it?" And I said, "Well, you know I have a goal to meet and I have my son" and that whole spiel. He said, "Oh, well, you know grad school isn't all about classes." I didn't say anything. He talked about conferences and asked how many papers I'd written independently, not counting the dissertation. And I said, "Well, none. I haven't written any papers and presented." He said, "Well, see, you're going to have a problem when you get out and try to find a job because there's a lot of students out there who are going to be on the ball with that and you're not going to be able to compete with that, because anybody can get a Ph.D. There's a difference between having a Ph.D. stamp and a Ph.D. level of education."

So I looked at him and said, "Really? Well, they get paid the same, don't they?" And he said, "Well if that's all you're concerned with, fine. But you can walk around with a stamp of a Ph.D. and not have a Ph.D. level of education. And I said, "Well, to me one person doesn't define what's a Ph.D. and what's not. Just like they call you doctor, they'll be calling me doctor and my paycheck will look the same, maybe more. So it doesn't make a difference to me." So then he said, "If that's your attitude, you can have it, but if you finish quickly like you say you will, I think that you're just prostituting the Ph.D." I looked at him and I said "Well, you just call me Dr. Ho' because I'm getting out of here like I said."

And the thing that really bothered me was that he was Black and I was Black and this is my naivete again, that people of color would stick with each other. It would bother me when a woman would say, "Why are you doing this? Now you know you can't do this." I think that's being stupid; why would a woman want to put another woman down? It bothered me when a Black person said the same kind of things, because if anything, anyone Black here knows how hard it is in this environment. If nothing else I want to get out of here. I want to get out of here as soon as humanly possible.

Graduate school, if nothing else, showed me that in life whatever you really want, you've really got to work for. It isn't even about knowledge: it's about who can last the longest. Who can really jump through these hoops and get the job done. If you can keep jumping through the hoops, you can do it. If you can stick with the plan, and stick to it when it seems like nothing else is working, and it seems like it will never happen because there are people in your way—but if you can still get around them or work through them somehow, then you get the prize. But other than that, no way. They'll get you every time. You've got to look out for you. There's no one else up there but you. And if you don't feel that way, I feel sorry for you.

JAMIE

I had been working for 30 years and I had always said, 30 years and I'm out of here because there are your political entities in other places as well as in the university. Well, when I got to 30 years, my kids were grown and I thought, I have invested all this time in my profession. I don't want to do something else but I do want to do something somewhat different. So that's why I went back. I'd always wanted a doctorate. I had started on one when I had our third daughter, so it was something that had been put off and put off and it also fit into the idea of wanting to do something different.

So in '92 I went back to grad school and of course everything I already did was too old. So I basically had to do all the coursework again because I had to update and then move on into the doctoral program. And I did the whole thing in three years. So that was pretty concentrated work. You know I was taking anywhere from 17–18 credits during the one year I took off from work, including a full load in the summer. When I got to writing my dissertation I kept my nose to the grindstone and finished in three years and one summer.

But during the program, I got an A in the course that was preparation to the initiation of the dissertation, but the administration told me that they really didn't want me to become a doctoral student. I think it was because I didn't have a master's degree and also it seemed that at my age I didn't fit their agenda. I think the department is very much interested in promoting themselves. If you are a person who comes in and somehow they think you will do things that are going to bring the department into the forefront as far as the United States is concerned or the world, they want you. And if you're older and you don't really look like you're going to contribute that much, then they don't want you. They were interested in what you could do for them, not what they could do for you. So I think they assessed that I probably was not going to do that much for the department and they decided they didn't want me to be there—which was crushing. So I felt very very badly about that.

I went and talked then with another professor in another program. And he said, "Well, you still need to do a practical experience because when you go to get a job, they're going to want to know that you taught at the university level." So he's the one who talked me into getting into an assistantship. And he was the one who said, "Hey, we want you" and brought me right into the program, ended up being the chair of my committee. I was given a lot of responsibility and my judgment was respected.

Well, let's go to my committee. It was hard to get a committee together because there weren't that many people in the department. One of my committee members was terrific, very supportive, but two of them were adversarial to each and I got caught in the middle. When it came time for me to get my committee together, I could not get the two men in the same room. I had to go in and talk to one separately and then I had to go meet with my committee.

And it was just a terrible struggle to get the person from outside the department, a terrible struggle. You know, it was just excuse, excuse, excuse, and he couldn't do it, he couldn't do it, he couldn't do it. And of course when he could do it, then I couldn't get the other two. It was awful. I had to go to his house. He was on vacation. It was just awful to try to get the four of them together and one of them wouldn't meet with the others at all. So I finally got the other three, and on the day of my defense one committee member said he could come but he'd be late and the other people could go ahead.

The other people chose to wait. So for over an hour the head of my committee was trying to keep me calm. You know what state you're in when you're going to defend your dissertation. And finally he came and the three of them met with me and one had already said he had some reservations and had written a lengthy reservation. The other three said that they accepted my work and that I was finished. So then the fourth committee person, who wouldn't come but had told me that he expected me to return and tell him what happened at the meeting, then I had to go back to him and tell him what all had happened. And I just was really upset. But I did get through and get my degree and I'm working at a college near here.

I'm still real good friends with one woman because I worked with her and she was one of the "in" people in my first department. And I've never told her my story but she talks about the different people that were in the program when we were there. And she'll say well, this one didn't finish and that one didn't finish, some other one didn't finish. And I'm thinking, isn't this interesting? All these people that the star professor picked out and figured they fit his agenda, they didn't even finish their degrees and here I've been published. You know, I won't fit his agenda. He didn't think I had enough to contribute to his plan. So it is interesting.

By the way, I met that professor the same weekend that I received my doctoral degree and he said, "Oh, how's your program coming?" I said I graduated yesterday. He said, "You what?" I said I received my Ph.D. yesterday. And he was just, his jaw was on the floor. I had to hold myself back from offering to pick it up for him. So it was like he underestimated me, and now, this month, I'm published.

SAM

I was always an outsider. I'm married, and we live a pretty good life, materialistically. I make money and my spouse makes money and so we didn't have to suffer the sort of traumas that most Ph.D. students do, never having any money. And so that was something that I didn't even ever have to deal with. I never had to pay tuition because I was on an assistantship and I always had plenty of money, I was able to go to conferences. Now that makes a difference because it causes some jealousy with students who can't afford to go to conferences. But they looked at it as, "Why is she missing class?" Even though the conference was really scholarship, if others couldn't do it, then they didn't want anyone else to do it, either.

The climate of the program is a climate of anger. It's a climate that privileges, definitely privileges, whiteness as a race. For instance, all the Hispanic graduate students, about ten of them, were in one office. Some were Cuban, some were Puerto Ricans, some were from Miami and they weren't just some group of generic Hispanics. The department head never did see that.

I think this is a traditional, conservative program that has no vision, no vision for anybody but mainstream suburban white students. I think the professors, most of them, lack any kind of social knowledge or commitment to social justice. There's never been, since I've been there, any kind of celebration of youth or students or children, never even an end of the year picnic or a getting to know you event. There's never an orientation at the beginning of the year for students to get to know each other. There is a punitive one-week orientation for graduate students in which they're required to go and sit. Basically they're told they won't get their funding if they don't attend this one-week meeting, and all it does is basically hit people on the head and make them learn names and humiliate them. It treats them like they're three years old. Politically, if you open your mouth you're alienated. You have no right to have an opinion, you're just a student.

My first year of teaching ended, and I registered for summer classes and wanted to teach summer school. All of a sudden I was told there were no summer school classes for me. When I inquired about this sudden lack, I was told that since I hadn't registered for summer classes in my department, I couldn't teach. Basically what they were saying was that until they got enough graduate students enrolled in summer courses that the regular faculty wanted to teach, I wouldn't be allowed to teach in the department. Basically there was a blackmail kind of thing going on: if you want to teach during the summer in our program, you must also be enrolled in the program's summer courses. In fact, there was actually a memo that came out to that effect. And so there were some students from Taiwan who were pretty meek and not challenging of the system forced to enroll in courses that they didn't want, basically because they were told that they could probably lose their funding if they didn't.

Politically there was a lot of stuff that went on constantly. Of course, everything is political. Everything is connected to everything else and so it's hard to differentiate. I found it a highly charged, highly political, highly conservative climate. A dean who was always kind to me would act like he'd listen but would end up going whatever way the wind was blowing. A chair that absolutely had no consciousness about graduate students, never learned their names, never welcomed them to the program or said goodbye to them when they got their Ph.D.s. A faculty that's very angry at each other, different factions not liking one another, a lot of gossip, a lot of anger, a lot of ownership of graduate students. For instance, my first department always maintains a huge number of graduate students, but the department I finally transferred to never had any graduate students, no graduate assistants whatsoever. The graduate students became the capital on which power structure was built in every department.

I see a lot of depression among the students, a lot of inability to finish. I've yet to see anybody go through with one committee. The amount of changing of committees is pretty incredible. For instance, the endowed chair had been sitting for the last three years on two students' committees. Because he took a semester off, he decided to resign from committees and left these students in a real mess. Really, there's no regard for students. There are endless arguments as to scheduling, with no accommodation and very little guidance for students. And yet the scrambling to have students' files in their offices when spring comes, because professors get paid more money for more advisees. So it's very important to have a lot of files in your office. Yet as soon as the spring evaluation is over, all of a sudden advisees are dropped again.

My own committee changed because my chair insisted on my doing what he wanted me to do and I didn't want to. Then, I decided I wanted females or people of color on my committee. When I realized there were no females because of how few females there are in this university and in this college, I had to get all males. I could have had two people of color, but basically I ended up opting for white men with power just—to be honest—just to get myself through because I saw how disenfranchised females and people of color are on committees.

One student who did finish her master's must have gotten her thesis turned back three or four times by one professor who would constantly make somewhat veiled racist remarks about her style of writing. She was Hispanic. He would always give her B+'s and A–'s whereas he gave all the white kids in the class straight A's. To this day, when she visits me, to this day she almost quivers when she talks about this man, and she's been graduated for two or three years. Students of color and gay or lesbian students seem to be the most mistreated and the next to them would be people who have opinions like me.

Nothing that looks like direct discrimination, though. For the gays, it's more defensive homophobia. I couldn't be very specific. There's one lesbian student, she's the one who left after three years without even finishing her candidacy and she felt like she was treated with homophobia. Basically she was a storyteller and sort of artsy and a colorful person, and her department didn't like her at all. They couldn't get rid of her fast enough. The students absolutely adored her. The undergraduates learned more from her than anyone. People wouldn't listen to her. I don't know if she'd say it was homophobia. I know that was part of it.

In a way, this is all funny. I think it's funny that this is a research institution with big-time prestige. I'm not impressed. I mean, I don't have any pride in getting my degree from this university. What I think of when I think of my degree is a hoop. A hoop I jumped through. No pride. I learned absolutely nothing from any class I took. I studied on my own, learned what I needed to learn, avoided professors I knew would be punitive and basically made my own program, used the resources I had and basically laid out what I wanted to do and did it. I can't imagine how horrible the program would have been if I did not have my decisions made and didn't know what I was doing. Because the agendas are so strong. The professors want you as a pawn. And I'm not one who was that way but I see my friends being caught. They're like flies in spider webs. They just can't get out.

ADRIAN

So we're starting the academic year, and one day the faculty supervisor of my assistantship comes to me and says, "Guess what: none of the professors wants to teach this course. Can you do it? It'll be really helpful for you." And I say, "Well, you know that I was offered an internship by someone outside the university I really want to work with," which was my big chance, and my supervisor knew this. But she says, "Don't worry. Teaching this class won't take up much of your time; we'll schedule this class on just one day." She had already gone above my head to my advisor and talked to him about it, and he thought it was a great idea.

So I'm saying, "Okay, fine."

Then she comes back another day and says, "It would be great—since you want to do a study on socialization—if you helped us out by doing this supervisory work for some students; it would give you some experience." So now, I'm up to teaching two courses, supervising some field experience for undergrads, and doing the internship I wanted to do with this other woman. Mind you: only two of the jobs were my choice, but I was up to all that. My supervisor kept telling me they'd work it all out so that my work for her only took up my Thursdays.

Now the semester starts. Everybody is supposed to be happy. And then she starts changing the assignments. And without telling me, she gives me seven undergrads to supervise. Do you know how I found out? From them—from the students. I was at one of the sites where I'm supposed to be a liaison, and the undergrads are saying, "You know, we're so happy to have you as our supervisor." And I'm like, "No, no, no. Hold on." So I speak to my supervisor and I say, "I heard that I have seven students, but you said that you and I were going to do five and five." And her answer is, "We can't do that now. You approved the document that I wrote about people's roles and responsibilities. You approved that handout." Now, I approved a handout that listed responsibilities. It certainly didn't say anywhere that I would have seven students to supervise.

"Is it really a problem?" she asks. "I need you." She really put me on the spot. I asked how I was supposed to supervise seven students when I was already teaching one course before she added the second one and I was doing an internship with someone else, too. Her answer was that I would just have to cut back and she advised me to tell the students that I could only see them on one day. And I said, "On one day? So I'm supposed to say "Well, I'll see you all on Monday." Seven of them? And then I told her "I can't do that. That's not ethical." But I obviously couldn't do the other internship.

She apologized, but I left there in tears. I didn't cry in front of her because I was so angry with her. Why couldn't she say, "I understand that this outside internship is important to your personal goals"? So I left there destroyed. And interestingly enough, when I called the outside person to tell her that I wasn't going to be able to do an internship with her, she said "I understand. I kind of figured this would happen"—which I thought was very interesting. It showed me that she had worked with university faculty enough to know this kind of shit would happen.

I tried talking to my advisor and the first thing that came out of his mouth was, "If she thinks that this whole program is going to survive because of the exploitation of graduate students, she's wrong." That's the first thing that came out of his mouth because he was pissed off because on top of everything else, my supervisor had me babysitting for her. He didn't think that was appropriate. I mean, he's had kids too and he's had undergrads that volunteered. He says, "Who needs a job? I may need somebody on Saturday." But he's never used graduate students he says, so when this happened he was really upset. But then again, he said, "What are you going to do?" And I said, "Since my supervisor's in charge of my scholarship, how can I say 'No. Screw you. I'm not supervising seven people, and I'm going to do the internship I want to do'"? I couldn't because she was in charge. So I dropped my internship, which sucks. Now mind you: I'm still trying to do my studying. So I'm still meeting with the people on my committee to get my studies started. And I don't know if you realize, but if you have seven students to supervise and you're teaching two other classes, there's no way.

So that was the beginning of the end because by the end of this semester I was completely overworked, I couldn't get anything started on my study because I had no time, and I knew my supervisor didn't care. Students and faculty members were supposed to work together as a collaborative effort, and what happened was that supervisor was just not a collaborative kind of person anymore. When I came here, she was. We taught a course together and we did everything in an even fashion. So for me, it was very hard because I saw her change as a person.

I don't know what happened. Promotion and tenure are the only things that divide the two times . . . and I guess the power. She became a leader of this project and I don't think she has those skills. I think she wanted to do this project, but I think she bit off way too much. One thing that she's very adherent to is the schedule. This has to be done by September, this by October, and when deadlines came up too fast she'd just make the decisions. She started making decision after decision and then just pissing everybody off because it was supposed to be a collaborative project. Finally someone in the project wrote an e-mail which was really raw and told my supervisor that they were tired of her pulling the wool over their eyes. It was really really nasty.

The supervisor, she's just not . . . I don't know, she's just not an honest person. One time, somebody told her I did something and she got all mad at me and was all upset with me until I said "No. That's not what happened. Why didn't you just ask me if it was true?" And then she apologizes and starts blaming it on a bunch of different things, like one time I came in jeans and sneakers for a lunch meeting with a student—and I wasn't even supposed to come in that day. She got mad at me for that. And then she tells me I'm undermining her, and then "No, no, no, I didn't mean undermining. I'm just under a lot of stress." Yeah? Well, we're all under a lot of stress. That's never been fixed for me, so I just kept working on the project to the best of my ability.

Previous to this episode she decided she was going to add another person on to help with the supervising load—but only then, when things were starting to go wrong for her. Not before, not when I needed her to get somebody else because I had an internship arranged for myself. So I worked out the rest of the year with three students to supervise, and I just did my job. I went in and I left and that was it.

I thought this was an opportunity to be a professional, and I thought that I was working towards the goals of this project, which is that the people we worked with outside the university and the university faculty could find a place to come together. I was really into the rhetoric of it and I really believed in it—and nobody else did. For me, it was just sad because I thought that I could be ethical at all times, and people were requiring me to be unethical. When I was honest and ethical with the people outside, basically other faculty members here would say "You have to watch what you say and you have to be careful with this and you have to be careful with that." I just didn't get it.

Everything I teach and everything that I am is about meaningful learning, and this is no longer meaningful to me. I can't write a dissertation about collaboration because this is bullshit. The university doesn't really care; they really don't value outside opinions. It's all bullshit. It's about universities using this as a new trend, a new source of money, so I can't write about that. Because what I want to write about is the truth and who is going to sign off on the truth?

Deciding to quit was a big deal. Like anything, of course, if you don't complete it after you thought you would, you feel like you failed. To get out of that feeling took me a long time. But I value myself enough to stop doing this to myself. That's the thing: I don't think I could stay another year here or work with these people anymore. I am just so completely disappointed at the level of, at the non-level of professionalism of the people here. You heard my story, the story of all the battles that I've gone through for my students because of the stupidity that goes on here for the sake of research. The thing is, I'm trying not to think of leaving the program this way. I'm trying to be a grownup and say "Okay, this has been an incredible learning experience"—but the reality is that I have three years of course work that mean nothing.

I don't value our program. All this happened just in the last semester, and still no one wants to change the program. I've been fighting about this for four years. And nobody cares because this is a research university and that's what we care about. Research. Not teaching, not educating people for tomorrow. And if you're not a kid who's getting all the money in the world and mom and dad take care of you, if you have to work full time or if God forbid you're a returning adult and have kids, there is no chance for you in this program. There's no chance for you. And that to me is just a million issues that I've taken up and nobody cares. The same thing with this big project. It's an elitist program. You have to be able to come here a month early and stay here through June and work full time. So how can you possibly work? I have kids, my students, that are cleaning houses, that are stuffing envelopes, that are working at the Student Center until midnight to make it without making a big deal about it because they were told that they couldn't work. So many issues are going on around here that I don't even know if I want to be affiliated with this university anymore.

That's how bad it's gotten. Before, I thought, this is important. I'll get a degree from this university. I was thinking in that mentality but now—no. I don't think I even want to associate myself with this situation because it's not right. So now my own ethics are being called into play and I'm thinking, "No, no. Can't do it. Not for a degree." So that's where I'm at.

Last week or the week before I had to say hi and ask my supervisor if she could write me a letter and I hated every minute of that. And you know what's funny is that I know she hates it too. Because I know she does not want to write a letter. She said she's already getting her secretary typing it up. But you know what I mean: I didn't feel bad only about myself. I just felt, this is stupid. She doesn't want to write a letter about me either. But what can you do? What can you do? I need a job.

COREY

Eleven years I've been in school. I worked until 1988, and then I got a little disgusted because I couldn't seem to get the promotions I wanted. I asked the supervisor, "Why is it that I'm not getting promoted?" I was training people and they were getting promoted. This was a civil service job, and I was a computer operator. And he sort of said, well maybe you need to take a few courses. I just quit working and started school full time that fall. And yes, I'm getting tired. I need a real job. I need a good job.

I knew school would benefit me some way, so I went back. The Dean of Arts and Letters mentored me and she pushed me on out to go to graduate school. I'd only planned to finish and get my master's and go back to work for the government. But I went to a conference and presented a paper and this one professor came up to me and said, "I have heard lots of papers and pretty good papers and I've been to lots of conferences, but your paper is a very good. I think you're Ph.D. material." So . . .

I had my bachelor's in English and my master's in English, and I was working on my Ph.D. in English here but I didn't pass my comps. And that was the first time I'd seen what people had been talking about, how political this organization is, academia.

I thought I had my committee. I sent letters out and they were all agreed that yes, they would be on my committee. I didn't know what the next steps were because strange enough, every department will do this comp thing differently. I didn't realize that I was supposed to have a separate reading list for each professor that each would approve or make some adjustments to and say to me, okay, concentrate on these particular people. So what happened was I put together this one, long, five-page, 90-some articles and books reading list, and I gave it to all four of the professors for their approval. And no one responded.

So I worked on the list for one year. I'm sure—I know I have copies of this—I sent each one of them a follow-up letter at three-month intervals, and then my advisor went on a Fulbright, to Spain I think. So he was gone. But he never responded one way or the other that the list was incorrect, that I should have done something different with this list.

When my advisor finally got back, he said, "This will not do. Is this just the list for me?" And I said no, this is everyone's. He told me I was supposed to split it up and give one part to each person. So now we're talking about one year that has passed. This had already been one year, from one November to another November. And I've got four crates of books and I'm trying to read through them. Plus I'm trying to teach, plus I'm trying to finish up a couple of courses that I think I'm going to need.

So anyway, after he came back, what I did was divide the lists up. And I'm telling you, no one else is responding even though I sent them letters and even e-mailed them. I gave him his separate list and I gave everyone else their separate list. No one else responded except him. I told one professor that I'd sent him e-mail and he told me that he had three hundred messages on his server and didn't know if I'd sent him e-mail or not.

Each time I gave my advisor a list, he would add to it. And finally his list became ninety-three items. I asked my advisor if he really expected me to read all that, and he said yes. When I went to talk to him and tell him what I was getting out of the articles and the books, he stopped me from talking and just talked to himself. The last time I tried to talk to him about one particular reading hoping to tie things together, he took out his pen and he started reading his mail. Right in front of me. He wasn't paying any attention to me.

As it turned out, I was getting real close to the exam and I asked for an extension, because after three years of being in the Ph.D. program you had to take your comps. I realized that there was a conflict between the woman in the graduate office and my advisor. I needed an extension and nobody was responding. She said to me that I needed to write a letter and explain why. My advisor told me something that I should never have done, and I knew that I shouldn't have done it, but he wouldn't sign off on the extension papers if I didn't. He wanted to see what I wrote in the letter of explanation. What he wanted me to do was blame everyone, basically, except himself. And he wanted me to be real specific in complaining about the other three professors who did not respond to my reading list or my letters.

I didn't feel comfortable with this because I was actually saying to professors, "You didn't do what I expected you to do so I've got to defer my comps because of you." It didn't look good and it didn't feel good. Still, I'm reading and he's telling me that he expects all those things done. So, I let him look at the forms and I sent the letter out he wanted.

I was in the middle of some conflict between my advisor and this graduate department person but I couldn't do anything about it. The graduate department woman's husband, who was on my committee, got so angry he went to my advisor and said he wouldn't serve on my committee. He was going to drop me. Two weeks before the exam! Well, nonetheless, I said, I'm going to take this exam. I knew I had two chances to take the exam so I set it up anyway.

I took the exam, went home to my own state, and got a letter in the mail. This is how I found out that I was out of the program. Not only did I not pass my comps, but I was out of the program without even having an opportunity to take the exam a second time. The letter said I was out, period. Period. The woman in the graduate office let my advisor know how much power she had by getting rid of me right away.

People were walking on egg shells around me because they thought, they really believed, I was going to fight it. I don't give up easy, okay? But what would be the point of staying here and having the same person—because he was my mentor—mentor me right out of the program again? I needed another hell? No. I thought I was being held under his wing and I wasn't. He dropped me like a bad habit. It was better for me to walk out of that bad situation, get away from it, from those two being at each other, the very nasty way they were at each other. If I were not the person that I am, I would probably have fallen apart. I probably would have. But I had the encouragement of friends, I mean really good friends, people who had known me since I'd been here, and my husband saying to me "We don't understand why you should leave. You can go into another department." And I did.

The way I learn is by experience. It was so easy to get into what I learned here, in the program I'm in now. When I was in that first department I kind of saw things, and I wanted to speak about my own experiences, but he would mute every woman's mouth. He would mute us by talking over us. He would do this to all, but the Black male students and his other students, he gave them respect, a respect that people should have all the time. But he never gave it to us. Sometimes we'd almost be saying the same thing and he'd give them more credit for having said it. It was very obvious. If you've ever been discriminated against as a woman, you can't really tell somebody how you know that they've done it but you know they've done it and so this is the kind of discrimination that was going on in the classroom all the time.

There were other Black women who were in this class and they would come to me because I'm an older student and they were like, what is wrong with him? Take the course since you're in there and then you'll know never to take him again, just never take another class from him.

I rarely had a good relationship with my female White professors, either. I don't know what it was. Not one thing that I can actually name, and different for me, because when I'm done being a student, I also like to say I'm your friend. There's some way oftentimes that you can bridge the two. But even in the Women's Studies classroom, I was one of three Black women in the classroom and the rest were White female and one White male. One time, they were doing stereotypes, it was some kind of exercise in what kind of stereotypes do you have for certain groups. So we had Jewish people, Hispanics, Black male, Black female. And then I raised my hand to these two white people, one was a teacher's assistant and the other was the professor, and I said "Why don't you have White female and White male on this list?" Whiteness was not even a part of the categories. And so while she was trying to uplift women, she was downplaying her whiteness and all White people.

Now in this new department, I've gotten so much encouragement. After failing those first comps, I was limping with my heart in my hand, so tender and so raw from all of this, and wondering if there was a way out. Now here, with this advisor, the first day we talked and I told him what my interest was and I'm thinking, "He really doesn't want to hear this," but I told him what my interest was and this man embraced me, I mean hugged me. It was like a show of sincerity to me even though in my mind I still said I don't know if I should believe this. He said it and he lived up to it from that day until June and taught me a way of teaching. Because taking his classes has taught me a new way of teaching. I don't have to pass down the stern English teacher demeanor to my students and be so hard, no giving and no taking. I used to say to my students, I would say to them, "You haven't been here long enough to know anything, so do all the work." Oh, the mistakes I made.

Thank God, I learned a different way. And one that was probably closer to my nature. I'm a nurturer and I know that's what I am. I'm firm. My children, I treated them with a firm, tough love attitude. The love was there in abundance and so when I saw this kind of thing being practiced right there with us graduate students, with grown people—well. You know, adults, we think we don't really need to be coddled and all this kind of thing, but actually we did need it. This man showed us how you have to have passion and a little interest in your students and a real interest in their learning before you can become the kind of teacher that you want to be.

My interest is Black women and how Black women interact with each other. That was what my master's thesis was about. And I wanted to continue that research. And so when my new advisor read my proposal, he loved it. It is a totally wonderful thing for me. It's like I'm doing this dissertation for my advisor in a way. I don't want to let him down. Not that I think I could, but I want to do it because I know that he validates me. He makes me feel like a whole person, a scholar. I don't know how much more rewarding that could be.

ALEX

I've always been a smart person and a good student, but I guess I had this image of graduate school as being the hallowed halls or ivory tower or something. Being a working-class girl, I wondered if I had whatever it took. Not just the smarts, but the savvy to handle graduate school. Really, I went through some serious thinking about that because . . . I think because of my working-class background. Was I going to be able to, not compete, but deal with highly intellectual people. I worried even though I knew I was as smart as any of them.

It's funny to look at it now, having had the education, and to remember how it was then. Now, I can put names to the struggle I was having; I thought I wouldn't have the kind of language that people have. I wouldn't have read the right books, studied the right philosophies or I wouldn't have the background of knowledge that other people coming into graduate school would have. I think about it now, and I think that one of the things that could have daunted me then was my age—but it didn't, not in the least. I thought, "I'm at a pretty cool age to do this." It was an "If not now, then when?" kind of thing. I was thirty-two and I really didn't have any doubt about that at all. My doubts were more personal: Did I have the intellectual wherewithal to be able to handle a place like this school? I didn't have a name for it; it just felt like generalized self-doubt. It came out as "Am I smart enough?" I couldn't intellectualize it anymore than that.

I started leafing through Peterson's catalog, *Peterson's Guide to Graduate School*. Somewhere, and I can't remember where, I heard that this school was number one in my field. Where I got that I can't tell you right now. But I started looking at this school. I was already familiar and once I realized they had this program that was all there was to it. I didn't apply anywhere else. I applied, got accepted, and that was it. By the beginning of January I was applying for grad assistantships and I didn't get one. My first year was self-funded.

When I was first accepted, I got a call from my advisor and we spent a good deal of time on the phone. I really liked talking to her, got along with her great. Then she quit and I was assigned a new advisor. I just left it at that because I was so busy getting ready to move and everything, I figured I'd see the new guy when I got there.

I started classes, and it got to be the first week of October and I still hadn't met my advisor. I tried to get in touch with him several times, and then I finally talked to his secretary and said "Look: I have to meet my advisor." So she gave me an appointment, but when I got there the man treated me like I'm somewhere maybe just up off the floor. He was talking down to me, and he actually said, "Well. How did you get to a place like this?" I guess he didn't approve of my sweats and sneakers. I don't know. I still don't know what reflection I gave off to make him say that to me.

Anyway, I said I came to him because I wanted to plan out my course of study. I guess it didn't dawn on me right at the time how condescending he was. I just wanted to get what I needed from the meeting. So we start talking about various courses and I raised my concern about funding, saying I was hoping for a graduate assistantship. Now, I had seen a posting for a graduate assistantship at the center he supervised, and so I started talking about how I might like to apply for that because it involved a lot of writing and I'm a good writer. He said to me, "That position is only for international students; don't bother applying." Nowhere on the notice did it say international students only—you can't say that. It's a job. It has to be open for whoever is the best qualified applicant. But he insisted it was only for international students in a way that sent the clear message "You are not good enough to work for me." I got it. So I packed up and left. And I started thinking about how he had treated me, like a low life. I got mad and I went and told the head of the department. I ended up being called for an assistantship in another area, which I kept until I finished my program—isn't that amazing? I wonder if it could have anything to do the fact that someone who happens to work in the Affirmative Action office told me I had real case of discrimination. Actually, I was hurt enough and mad enough that when I found out I had a case I seriously thought about taking action. But then the other assistantship came along, so I decided to let it go. I couldn't prove the sudden job was a kind of bribe, and I got what I needed. So I let it go.

It's interesting how the guy's bias toward international students played out, though. There was a woman in the program who was from Hawaii, but she is a Caucasian woman who had transplanted twice and married a Hawaiian man. She was the one who eventually got that first assistantship. I guess she was sufficiently exotic. I guess to be international and exotic enough for him, you have to fly over water to get there.

I do think that in the end, despite the advisor problem, I was luckier than most people as far as my assistantship went. I never felt like I was being abused. I've heard the horror stories of other people having to teach full teaching loads and then also try to do their own thing. That didn't happen to me.

By the end of my first semester, though, I was really asking "What the hell have I done?" Moving anywhere is a difficult adjustment, but I looked around the school and the town and it was so obvious that the place is really cut out for the eighteen- to twenty-two-year-olds. And here I was, thirty-two at that point, almost thirty-three, and I felt maybe I just didn't belong. The person I had been living with had refused to move with me, so we had broken up and I had that on my mind. And then I face things like an advisor who makes it oh-so-clear he doesn't want me in his program. So there was a point where I seriously considered quitting. One night I was teaching a class and enjoying the discussion, but all the problems were really weighing on me. On break, I went to the vending machine and this other faculty member was there getting coffee or whatever. He looked at me, asked how I was doing—and I burst into tears. I told him. I told him I was thinking of quitting, and why, and how I was questioning whether grad school was for me. He took me outside, told me I couldn't quit, and really gave me a pep talk. I felt this kind of kinship from him because I'd already talked to him enough to know that he came from the same sort of background that I did, a working-class background. He basically talked me into staying, and to this day I thank him for that. Just knowing someone around here to whom I could relate, who understood the same kind of emotional and intellectual struggles that somebody like me goes through in a university setting meant a lot.

Probably the biggest power struggle, or political struggle, I encountered turned up during the hearing on my dissertation proposal. Of all things, it came from the guy who had talked me into staying in school. He and another member of my committee are very supportive of working-class students and critical ideas and all of that. I think they used my proposal hearing as a time to show off to each other how much they knew about critical theory and about the kind of issues that I was dealing with in my proposal. The entire hearing was dominated by a discussion of theory that ensued between the two of them. They would argue some obscure fine point of critical theory in a realm I wasn't even familiar with, and then they'd bounce the ball over to me and of course I couldn't answer their question. I was getting very upset, and I felt very dominated. In the end I felt very criticized and almost belittled. Afterwards, I cried because I felt like those two had just really taken it over.

Then, on top of all that, I knew that a third member hadn't even read my damn proposal until the day before the hearing. He hadn't given it a careful reading. It would have been nice for him to read it and give me feedback and let me be prepared to answer the kind of questions that he was going to throw at me. "How can you improve this draft to include thus and such?" Those kinds of things. No, for him it was more like, "I'll use this as an opportunity to tear her down in front of other people in the department." The other people on my committee included the department head and some more senior faculty, so this guy decided to show off. And even my strongest supporter played into it because he loves a good intellectual debate. I felt really powerless afterward.

I pointed out to them at some point that it was just before Christmas break and I was supposed to be doing data collection in January, so I needed to get their issues straightened out. They approved my proposal, but contingent upon decisions to be made at another meeting the next day. What I did was go home that night prepare my rebuttal—for their behavior in the proposal hearing. I went into that meeting the next day and really let them have it. I just told them how I felt powerless, how I felt like I wasn't being given full consideration. They actually listened to what I had to say and felt bad about it and ended up wanting to make me feel better about the whole process. Afterwards everything straightened out.

This was probably a highlight of my experience: in my most powerless moment I spoke back with power.

CHAPTER 7

How Might Things Be Otherwise?

*Ah, but a man's reach should exceed his grasp,
Or what's a heaven for?*

—ROBERT BROWNING

The point of a critical analysis is to uncover how power relationships work in unequal arrangements, making explicit the implicit mechanisms that function to support the status quo at the expense of some oppressed group or groups. For those interested in social justice, the hope is that oppressors—who are often unaware of their privileged position and its impact on others—will, once their awareness has been increased, act in more just ways. A second hope is that the oppressed—who are often equally unaware of their own manipulation and their own potential—will, once they better understand hegemonic practices, realize their own power and act to change conditions they begin to perceive as unacceptable. As part of a body of work founded on critical theory, then, this text shares the common goal of enabling transformation—of thought and action both:

> [It] aims at promoting critical consciousness, and struggles to break down the institutional structures and arrangements which reproduce oppressive ideologies and the social inequalities that are sustained and produced by these social structures and ideologies. (Van Manen 1990, 167)

Work embodying a critical perspective is about change: about identifying gaps between the ideal and the real and trying to move the latter closer to the former.

Often, when this point is made in a critical discussion, readers or listeners who think of themselves as highly in tune with the real world and as pragmatic jeer at critical theorists as impractical, unrealistic idealists.

Essentially, critics most often do not believe that humans are simply going to say "Oh, well, yes, you're right. I have been privileged at others' expense. I'll just hand off some of this power to folks whose interests may be different from mine." Damrosch, one of the academy's keenest critics, makes precisely this charge against many would-be reformers (1995):

> It is interesting to observe how often critics of academia spend much of their time detailing professorial venality, sloth and indifference, only to turn around in conclusion and call for changes that would require the professors suddenly to become exceptionally altruistic, energetic, and caring. (164)

His point, alas, is well taken. Many in the academy will, no doubt, never interest themselves in improving conditions for others—especially for students, whose place in the institutional hierarchy is so low.

To grant that point, however, does not rule out the possibility of change, as should be evident by the growing number of thoughtful critics who have been working to call attention to problems in the enterprise and to spark reform (M. Anderson 1996; Baird 1990, 1993a, 1993b; Bowen & Rudenstine 1992; Damrosch 1995; Hanson 19921 Heinrich 1991, 1995; Kerlin, B. 1995; Kerlin, S.P. 1995a, 1995b; Smith 1990; Tierney 1991, 1992; Willie, Grady & Hope 1991; Ziolkowski 1990). While some of the powerful will, no doubt, never change, there are indications that a significant core of thoughtful, ethical members of the academic community in a variety of roles perceive the need for change and are willing to engage in the struggle to accomplish it. It is to such cultural workers that this work hopes to speak.

Effecting change in an institution still directly tied in many ways to a Middle Age mentality will be no small feat. If we are to make any progress at all, we must begin with trying to imagine how things might be different.

> So strong is the hold on our minds and imaginations of what is that to make substantial change in the way we think about the whole process of education will require, in David Bohm's words "an energy, a passion, a seriousness, beyond even that needed to make creative and original discoveries in science, art, or in other such fields." (Smith 1990, 305)

If we can't imagine an alternative reality, we certainly can't pursue one. We need to explore, first, how might things be different? Then, we can ask what strategies we might use to pursue new goals.

How Might Things Be Otherwise? 137

This chapter intends to provoke our imagination by asking what we might seek to change and by offering a survey of possible starting points for reform. These possibilities range from minor changes that would at least immediately ease the suffering of many graduate students to significant re-vision of the entire enterprise, one that might help the academy move toward a democratically reconstituted vision of its own mission, goals and responsibilities.

RECENT THOUGHTS ON REFORM

Several analysts and writers who have detailed weaknesses in the current structure of graduate education have also formulated a variety of plans for its reform. These plans range widely in their visions of what's needed, from some tinkering with elements of the current system to fully reconceptualizing and reconstructing the entire enterprise. An overview of some of the most well known of these plans, offered in the next few paragraphs, offers substantive food for thought. It also reveals common concerns that provide practical starting places for reform, as will be detailed in the next section, along with their relationship to concerns raised in this text.

Perhaps the work that has gotten most respect and attention is Bowen and Rudenstine's massive study (1992), which Damrosch (1995) appropriately characterizes as a seminal work: "any contemporary analysis of graduate education must begin from their discussion and from the wealth of data they have assembled" (143). Based on their "wealth of data," these authors identify two essential problem areas they believe must be addressed: (1) funding and (2) the internal characteristics of programs (269–289).

Specifically, Bowen and Rudenstine suggest that in part we need to analyze the form and timing of funding for students—should teaching and research assistantships continue to function as funding mechanisms, and if so, to what extent and at what point in the student's work? They find this concern secondary, however, to a critical need to secure adequate funding for graduate students from a variety of sources, including the institutions themselves, the federal government, and foundations. Suggestions about program characteristics, which the authors characterize as "relevant mainly for programs in the humanities and related social sciences" and "intended to stimulate further discussion" (280), include rethinking: appropriate program size and content; program norms and content (especially those that affect time-to-degree); faculty advising; mentoring, reporting and accountability; and time-limited doctorates. Many of these concerns are echoed in other reports.

Lipschutz (1993), for example, lists seven specific areas for reform. Those also mentioned by Bowen and Rudenstine include advising and mentoring, financial support, curriculum (program content), tracking progress (reporting and accountability), and the need to streamline program practices and procedures. In addition, this report insists that institutions need also to think more stringently about their admissions policies and about institutional climate. Baird (1990), too, mentions funding as a critical issue and suggests that degree structure and requirements need to be re-examined, especially in light of factors that studies show inhibit student progress toward the degree. Advising also proves an issue in Baird's work, prompting him to suggest also that students be linked with advisors very early on in their program, that the institution encourage interaction among faculty and students, and—tellingly—that the institution find a way to ensure that all graduate faculty are familiar with its graduate programs and policies.

In her ten suggestions for lowering ABD rates, Hanson (1992, 12–16) provides another voice calling for improved funding for graduate study and, attending to common weaknesses in advising and funding, suggests also that students be encouraged to avoid full-time work before their dissertation is finished, and to select chairs and committee members carefully. She also suggests that faculty need to be particularly supportive of female students. Hanson's work, however, attends more to suggestions for how students might survive in the existing system than to ideas for serious reform, exploring such topics as dissertation logs and computer skills.

Ziolkowski (1990), Damrosch (1992), and Smith (1990) offer perhaps the most radical suggestions for reconceptualizing graduate education and the institution's related responsibilities. Their work addresses more theoretical, more slippery issues having to do with institutional climate and ethos, and it cannot be easily summarized in this overview. Their provocative thinking will, therefore, be presented in detail after a closer look at the common concerns identified by the researchers surveyed above.

CONSENSUS ON PRACTICAL CONCERNS

Among the wide variety of reports and analyses related to graduate education in recent years, consensus seems to emerge regarding some areas of critical and widespread concern: funding, accountability, advising and mentoring, and expectations. Each offers a potential starting place for

How Might Things Be Otherwise? 139

those who care about the quality of the lived experience of graduate school for students.

Funding

Among the most troublesome areas for graduate students clearly is funding, as several of the above-mentioned researchers note. Baird, for example, cites Bowen and Rudenstine (1992) in making this point in his own work:

> Graduate students often need financial support. Research suggests that graduate students who must rely on their own resources take one-half to two-thirds more time to complete their degrees than students with institutional support. Institutional support usually has a positive effect above and beyond the amount paid, in that it involves students in laboratory, research, and classroom activities. (Baird 1996, 27)

Even as they are careful about what the data in their study can and cannot be said to demonstrate, on this point Bowen and Rudenstine have no doubt that funding—and the form in which it is offered—make a critical difference to graduate students:

> For all of their limitations, these data clearly indicate both the differences in the basic structure of financial support between broad fields and the critical roles played at the present time by personal resources and university funding. To expect students to cover more of the costs of graduate education out of personal resources, would be to put at risk both the number and quality of candidates for doctorates. Such an approach would also make it even more difficult to include within the professoriate any significant representation of minority groups or, indeed, any significant number of individuals from families of modest means. The potential effects on the character and quality of teaching within the nation's entire educational system—and the subsequent effects on so many aspects of national life—are strong reminders of the need to maintain effective programs of financial aid at the graduate level. (Bowen & Rudenstine 269–70)

Willie, Brady and Hope also make the point that, if institutions are genuine about their interest in democratizing the graduate student body—of working toward a more inclusive society and eliminating the category of

Other in the academy—then funding is a critical factor in pursuing this goal (1991):

> Full financial support from the first through the fourth or fifth year of graduate study probably would shorten the period of study and increase the degree-completion rate of black scholars. Foundation sponsorship is essential since African-American graduate scholars, by their own testimony, have limited access to campus-based sources of funding such as research and teaching assistantships. (75)

We must end our hypocrisy. We cannot continue loudly and publicly endorsing inclusive goals while we simultaneously deny the Other equal access to financial aid.

For this to happen, institutions must both pay more attention to the extent to which they fund students who constitute the academy's Other, and they must continue to invest heavily in their graduate students while also actively pursuing funds from other sources:

> Graduate education should not be seen as a "poor cousin" of either undergraduate education (which always has a stronger alumni/ae constituency) or research (which is more visible, and which often attracts outside funding more readily). Hard as it will be, especially under straitened financial conditions, educational institutions must continue to invest significant amounts of their own unrestricted funds in the support of graduate students. But not even the most determined effort to assign graduate education a high priority will permit adequate funding from institutional sources alone. Costs are too high, and competing priorities are too compelling. External funders must help much more generously, we believe, than they do at present. (Bowen & Rudenstine 269–70)

These researchers argue that increased funding from foundations and the federal government must be aggressively pursued—as the AAU 1998 report also argues. Such efforts are unlikely to be particularly effective, however, until they are formulated less in terms of self-interest and more in terms of moral and civic responsibility.

In line with this, institutions must stop using a critical student need for funding as an excuse for exploiting research and teaching assistants. This is not to say that assistantships should be eliminated, as some critics, like Martin Anderson, would argue. Instead, they must be designed to offer students benefits—such as the chance to grow through professional experiences—that institutions currently tout loudly but infrequently provide. Job assignments must be structured so that learning is an overt and critical element of TA and RA duties, not so that they provide the university with a maximum workforce at the lowest possible price. A bright spot in this area is that at least one effort is currently under way to accomplish just this goal:

> As an approach to improving this situation [i.e., that students are not prepared for most faculty activities besides research], a number of universities have developed programs to introduce graduate students to the full range of faculty life. The Preparing Future Faculty (PFF) program administered by the Council of Graduate Schools and Association of American Colleges and Universities with funding from The Pew Charitable Trusts, is perhaps the most extensive of these. Fifteen clusters have been formed, each comprising a research university and a diverse group of institutions such as a comprehensive university, a four-year liberal arts college, and a community college, all situated so that students can move easily among them. Doctoral students participate, on a discipline basis, in faculty activities in all four types of institutions. This program deals with the realities of being a faculty member in the variety of settings that constitute the academic job market. (La Pidus 1998, 99)

Here, the program is designed to provide students with a variety of experiences—not simply teaching the same entry level courses over and over and over or doing grunt work in someone else's research project—that can both help them grow as teachers and become more specific about the teaching environment that might best suit them in the future. The academy may benefit from their work, but so do the students who receive a great deal of information and experience related to career possibilities.

In an all-too-literal sense, institutions need to stop simply talking about finances in relation to student welfare (as opposed to institutional welfare), and to direct their energy, their focus, and their resources more intently toward that goal. Students, as well as institutions, must genuinely benefit from financial aid offered in the form of assistantships.

Accountability

As is true for the need for increased funding, there is no doubt that increased accountability in graduate education is long overdue.

> Students and institutions invest innumerable years, enormous energy, and massive amounts of financial resources in doctoral programs. Yet

> there is comparatively little accounting for what happens at many of the most critical junctures. In previous eras, when most programs were small and when candidates were relatively few, the individual apprentice-system was a plausible model. But given the totally new system that has evolved since the 1960s—particularly its heterogeneity, scale, comparative lack of funding, and decreased effectiveness in terms of completion rates and time-to-degree—the time for sensible modification seems overdue. (Bowen & Rudenstine 265)

Students need to know the average time-to-degree for a particular program as well as its completion, ABD and attrition rates, rarely available now. This would constitute a sort of truth in advertising standard for graduate programs, providing information far more useful to prospective students than how many graduate students were undergraduates in the Ivy League—especially if half of all students accepted to a program (from the Ivy League or not) routinely leave without completing doctorates. Much more systematic study and accurate information is needed than is now available.

Given the widespread agreement that faculty advising is a critical issue and that the dissertation phase is a particularly dangerous one for students, accountability in terms of dissertation advising seems a particularly acute need. Again, Bowen and Rudenstine aptly summarize the conclusion that several researchers have drawn (1992):

> Students and institutions invest massive amounts of time and other resources, and it seems only reasonable that there be standards of collective accountability that are both explicit and consistently applied.... [I]t does seem to be the case that few programs (if any) maintain careful and continuous records concerning faculty performance in dissertation-advising, and that effectiveness in this sphere usually counts for very little in the evaluation of faculty members when annual salary increases or even promotions are taken into account. Whether a faculty member has many, few, or no dissertation advisees; whether the students ever complete their dissertations, or complete them in a reasonably timely way; whether the advising process has been structured well and has been reasonably satisfactory—there is little or no documentation on these and related matters in most programs. It seems odd at best that the culminating aspect of the doctoral program should be subject to so little serious evaluation and monitoring, and that faculty members should not be more accountable. (14, 262–3)

How Might Things Be Otherwise? 143

As long as the institution values and rewards research and publication at the expense of teaching, advising, and mentoring, there will be little incentive for programs to pay attention to the experience of their graduate students. And, since productive faculty interaction has been identified as a critical element in completing the degree, institutions that genuinely care about the quality of their programs must develop accountability systems that effectively support high level faculty attention.

Advising and Mentoring

The lack of accountability makes possible a system in which advisors can ignore, misinform, bully, threaten or exploit their graduate students at will. Not only is accountability among the most critical of concerns for those wishing to build more effective programs, but it is also an ethical imperative. Faculty routinely abuse their absolute power over students, and an institution that allows such abuse is abdicating its moral responsibility.

There is, however, a central problem here, as Damrosch pragmatically notes (1995):

> No exhortations to change will have any effect on graduate education if the faculty do not wish to make the change. (140)

Accountability is the first step—but before an institution will be able to move the faculty to better serve students, it must offer the faculty a reason to do so.

> Traditionally, chairing six dissertations has been considered the equivalent of teaching one three-unit class. The units can then be "banked" and eventually redeemed for released time from teaching. Most profs would tell you, however, that this is mighty meager compensation for the amount of work involved in supervising dissertations. (Hawley 1993, 6)

Institutions, then, must overhaul reward systems so that effective mentoring becomes a goal that faculty will choose to pursue. After accountability systems have developed, departments must ensure that each faculty member has few enough advisees to allow for intensive mentoring. With better conditions, there is much that faculty might do to provide better service to students.

A related and depressingly easy task, as Baird (1996) suggests, is simply to be sure that all faculty understand program and university requirements and deadlines, so that they can provide accurate and clear information to students with questions. Beyond being informed about essentials, faculty might be encouraged to create opportunities for informal interaction with and among students as part of their mentoring activities. This is particularly the case for students who fall into Other categories and who feel most disconnected and excluded from the institutional community. Similar to advice that Hanson (1942) offers women, Willie, Grady and Hope (1991) offer advice that would benefit all students immensely:

> [T]his study indicates that predominantly white colleges and universities must undertake deliberate efforts to make the campuses of graduate schools more hospitable to African-American and other minority scholars. Inservice education programs are needed to help white faculty members learn how to serve effectively as mentors for minorities. Moreover, black and other minority students need increased opportunities to serve as research and teaching assistants with faculty. In general, the black scholars in this study said that opportunities to collaborate with faculty in intellectual activities outside the classroom were inadequate.
>
> One step that can be taken to promote the development of mentoring relationships is to encourage faculty to reach out to students through informal contacts, such as dinners for new students in faculty homes. The institution should also be flexible in approving student requests to change advisors if a student had identified a particular professor with whom he or she wishes to work. Random assignment of new students to faculty advisors is not likely to accomplish much more than perfunctory advisory duties, such as orientation to university procedures, approving study plans, advising on course selections, and so forth. Students should also be encouraged to take independent study or field experience course work that involves collaboration with both university and community contact persons. It is conceivable that mentors might come from the community setting, which, while not a source preferable to the university faculty . . . might create valuable professional contacts in the larger community. (76)

All students need to meet, know, and interact frequently with faculty. All faculty should be helped to understand how best to work with graduate

How Might Things Be Otherwise?

students in general as well as more specifically with students who have backgrounds that vary from the white, male, heterosexual, young, middle-upper class background.

In short, faculty must be encouraged to invest special attention and effort into the goal of creating coherent community for students, where students feel valued and supported. This is likely to prove a challenging goal, however, since it runs counter to the patriarchal system operating on a survival of the fittest model:

> Communal, collaborative, and nurturing ways of thinking and interacting—often associated with women—are antithetical to the old network, but if widely practiced among academics they could help heal the rifts between class, gender, and power. Although academia accepts the idea of women faculty, it does not accept women's ways of thinking and/or women's values. (Tokarczyk & Fay 1993, 8)

While this goal is likely to be resisted, especially by those who believe that because they suffered others should now suffer, it is essential that a more humane treatment of students be encouraged.

Since it is not to be expected (as Damrosch noted) that all faculty will blithely agree to more equitable power arrangements and an increased concern for student welfare, many are suggesting that the absolute power an advisor commonly wields in relation to a student be dispersed among several faculty:

> Still another approach involves attempting to alter fundamentally the "apprenticeship" model Thus, a number of graduate programs have recently moved to "committee systems," in which the dissertation prospectus, the research-plan, and progression-steps are reviewed by a small group of faculty members who are committed to the plan and to the student. This approach helps to ensure that no one faculty member will have exclusive control over the process, and it also helps to ensure that the student feels responsible to a set of faculty members, who schedule actual meetings with him or her, at agreed-upon times along the way. The committee system will probably not work for all programs—and it has its own particular hazards. But it does seem to work well at several institutions and it goes some distance toward ameliorating the "isolation" problem, the total exclusivity of the apprentice-pupil arrangement, and the tendency on the part of everyone to forget that the dissertation-phase should be thought of as something for

which the faculty as a whole continues to have joint responsibility. (Bowen & Rudenstine 1992, 262)

In some way, the future of a graduate student must be removed from the complete control of a single faculty member, as is now too often the case.

Implementing new systems of accountability will, as noted above, inevitably suggest new systems of rewards. For accountability reports to be perceived as important documents within an institution's culture, consequences must be attached to various levels of performance. As such consequences—rewards for valued behavior, for example—are made explicit, institutional expectations both for its programs and its people will need to change. For example, few (if any) institutions currently have explicit statements about expected time-go-degree or retention rates. If departments must begin keeping records about their performance in those areas, however, those reports will be taken seriously only if there is a system of rewards and/or disincentives in place for departments whose performance exceeds or falls short of institutional expectations. As faculty become more interested in these consequences, the institution will have to become increasingly clear about its expectations in all accountability areas. Of course it is unlikely that anyone would endorse inflexible guidelines, but some parameters—like an average time-to-degree of 4–6 years—can certainly be identified and become part of explicit institutional norms.

Expectations

For programs. In line with the need for less absolute control by individual faculty, there is a need for institutions, departments, and programs to be more explicit and less whimsical about what exactly is required of students.

> Doctoral programs do not "run themselves." Much depends on the care with which they are designed and the expectations that are established concerning the character and quality of work to be done by those admitted. The degree of structure built into the system is also very important. Under this heading, we include the clarity with which guidelines concerning the completion of requirements are communicated, the firmness with which they are enforced (always allowing for the intelligent application of general rules to individual cases), and the extent to which the performance of students and faculty alike is monitored. (Bowen & Rudenstine 1992, 250)

How Might Things Be Otherwise?

While this suggestion—that requirements should be clear and explicit—seems simplistic (like the suggestion that faculty must understand their own programs), it is still an important one in relation to students' ability to progress expediently. In line with this goal, unnecessary complexity (often the stuff of which reputation is made) needs to be removed from requirements:

> [G]raduate schools and faculty would have to look anew at the practices and procedures governing graduate education with an eye to making them as simple, helpful and effective as possible. (Lipschutz 1993, 74)

Such a goal, with an interest in adjusting procedures to students' best interests, might be far more useful than its obvious nature might suggest.

Rethinking program expectations in such a way would include rethinking the dissertation format with the goals of reducing inappropriate length expectations, exploring whether the traditional dissertation provides the most productive culminating activity for doctoral students, and considering the possibility of new forms of terminal degrees. Damrosch, for example, introduces some thoughts on substitutions for traditional format (1995):

> Our current students' needs may be better served by a much more open and flexible form of the dissertation. A student might benefit most from writing three or four separate articles in two or three different areas, with a different advisor for each, perhaps writing one or more chapters in collaboration with other students.... Why should the dissertation be presumed to be a protobook rather than a series of articles, each produced independently, sharing a common general theme or approach rather than developing a single argument? (162)

Given that journal articles are much more common writing activities for most researching faculty than books, and given that dissertations are not in the format common to books that are actually published, why not indeed?

Moreover, expectations for the amount of time it *should* take to write a dissertation as well as for the length a dissertation *should* reach need to be significantly adjusted in cases where the institution or department insists on clinging to the dissertation format. Ziolkowski (1990) believes that it's entirely possible that the current preference for weighty dissertations that take years and years to complete may be linked much more directly to the institution's desire to hire faculty with extensive job training than to any genuine benefit to students. His characterization of the situation is both apt and memorable:

> Some social scientists and most humanists bring quite different expectations to the degree. Many regard graduate school not simply as the place to acquire a certain level of knowledge and proficiency in a field but as an open-ended status where the aspiring Ph.D. can sit and "mellow" (like a wine?), "ripen" (like a cheese?), and "grow" (like a vegetable?)—the organic metaphors flourish in the prose of departments seeking more time and support for their students.... These expectations ... are still all too often implicit today in the expectations of departments interviewing candidates for their positions. How often is the gifted scholar, who has worked hard to complete the degree in a reasonably short time, passed over for the more "mature" candidate, who has acquired years of teaching experience while laboriously grinding out his or her four hundred pages? ... The correlation between time-to-degree and dissertation length makes the skeptical dean sometimes suspect that the dissertation is long because the "ripening" time needs to be filled out, and not vice-versa.... (192)

If student benefit were valued more than institutional benefits, such "ripening" would not be perceived as necessary or desirable, and time-to-degree as well as retention might well improve.

Another result of extensive problems with the current dissertation system has led others to start asking whether the Ph.D. itself ought to stop functioning as the "union card" for university faculty; perhaps, they suggest, degree designations should be revised to better indicate whether the candidate is more interested in a career emphasis on teaching or on research—or perhaps we should simply stop requiring the Ph.D. of university faculty because it does so little to develop good teaching skills. Hanson, for example, outlines some possibilities in these areas (1992):

> If a student's goal is to become a better college teacher, then a talent development argument would be that this student needs to focus on teaching rather than some lengthy research project. In such cases, students would receive ABD status upon completion of a given number of hours of coursework. Other alternatives would be to consider the C.A.G.S. (certificate of advanced graduate study) or the C. Phil (candi-

How Might Things Be Otherwise? 149

date in philosophy). Further inquiry needs to be made to see if alternative degree distinctions would serve the doctoral student's best interests. The Doctor of Arts, a non-research oriented degree that focuses on pedagogical methods, is another alternative that should be investigated. (16)

All such possibilities require a good bit of imagination on the part of members of the academic community. Whether we can meet the challenge of seeing such new possibilities as realistic, however, depends on whether we can be equally imaginative about changing our expectations for people as well as for programs. It's possible that changing what we expect of people will prove an even more challenging task.

For people. To enable the changes needed in faculty behavior and to dethrone the tortured dissertation as a necessary culminating experience, the academy's expectations in relation to faculty research and publishing will have to be significantly altered as well. The insistence on counting publications and using the resulting sum as the most critical factor in tenure and promotion decisions will have to stop. Contrary to popular myth, however, the demise of this expectation would be a benefit rather than a loss:

> ["Research"] has been made into such a comprehensive term that it now includes the most routine and pedestrian labors as well as the most brilliant original work. It is, of course, a major contention of [my work] that the routine and pedestrian far outweigh the brilliant and original; that routine and pedestrian research is not merely a very expensive nullity but a moral and spiritual drag on the institutions in which it takes place and a serious distortion of the nature of both the intellectual and the scholarly life. The economic cost is also scandalously high, if only because the less teaching a teacher does, the lower the general quality of teaching, the more huge classes, teaching assistants, etc., the higher the cost of the teaching that is done. If a professor teaches, say, one course in a session, a quarter, or a term, instead of three, his/her "cost effectiveness" is one-third of what it would be if he/she taught three. In other words, a high price is paid by the system for the time spent in research. (Smith 1990, 179)

Few faculty members or administrators would deny the validity of Smith's observations in private. It is time for academicians to openly acknowledge what they frequently say behind closed doors: that much of what passes for research is neither genuinely new nor useful. It is time for institutions to begin discouraging instead of encouraging meaningless publications that inflate an institution's research productivity.

Changes in research expectations for faculty are inextricably linked to hiring decisions—which are themselves inextricably linked to research expectations for new Ph.D.s. Attention will need to be paid to revising all of these areas for any single change to be effective, as Ziolkowski notes (1990):

> None of these changes can take place until the hiring departments modify what literary critics call their horizon of expectations.... If the expectations do not change, the system will produce more and more A.B.D.s and an inadequate number of Ph.D.s for the future. Departments should be seeking neither the scholar who has "ripened" long enough in graduate school to have compiled a five-hundred-page (and therefore probably poorly supervised) dissertation nor the scholar who has "matured" long enough to have acquired years of teaching or research experience (and therefore probably a corresponding sense of bitterness at having been exploited by the graduate institution). Departments should instead be happy to appoint well-trained young Ph.D.s who have demonstrated their commitment by moving expeditiously through a reasonable program to a degree that certifies their competence to begin a career in teaching and scholarship. (194)

Substituting common sense expectations for the worship of graduate school suffering and research mania will be no easy task: "The chief obstacle to structural reform in the system is the fact that most of the people now in it are products of that system" (Damrosch 142). But however difficult the challenge of changing expectations, the task is essential.

PHILOSOPHICAL CONCERNS

While many of the suggested changes above might improve the experience of graduate students, they do not satisfy the critical educator, whose goal is not to make an oppressive situation less painful, but to pursue a genuinely democratic society. The critical educator hopes to foster a new, more just and more humane worldview to guide all day-to-day practices. From this perspective, while the reforms outlined above might

How Might Things Be Otherwise?

be useful in the short term, they will not fundamentally affect the quality of life in graduate schools. For that, much larger changes are needed.

> No one approach or set of recommendations can expect to erase a dropout rate of 49% and more, but no reforms in graduate education are worth contemplating unless they give promise of making at least some improvement in the present situation. Bowen and Rudenstine's study offers a variety of recommendations, but these are geared chiefly toward helping the present system work more smoothly: streamlining requirements, improving funding, and generally reducing the time to degree. My own belief is that more substantial changes are needed. These changes will involve modifications to program requirements, but such reforms must accompany more basic shifts in the entire culture of graduate education. (Damrosch 147)

We endorse Damrosch's conclusion here: what is needed are "more basic shifts in the entire culture."

In essence, what is needed is a reconceptualization of graduate education. We must begin attending to the lived experience of everyone engaged in graduate education, and we must begin valuing graduate education as a *human* enterprise, rather than an institutional enterprise linked to income and prestige. So deep are the roots of the empiricism and rationalism that nourish the status quo, however, that concern for the emotional and spiritual health of the academy's members will seem hopelessly idealistic. And yet, some ethical educators have already risked being called cranks by their colleagues by outlining the need for just such a goal.

Hawley notes the reluctance of the professoriate to address such issues because they are alien or antithetical to the academic training most current professors experienced (1993):

> It is the *subjectively painful* experiences that underline most students' decision to quit, yet many doctoral faculty refuse to concern themselves with what they see as non-cognitive matters. Curiously, the higher they rise in their professions, the more cerebral some become and the more disparaging of the emotional components of learning. (20)

This refusal to acknowledge the non-cognitive as essential components of experience has a devastating effect on those engaged in the enterprise.

By the time a student is well into a program and wholly dependent upon advisor and committee, his or her world view has been not just changed, but warped:

> Things are cold as ice—dry ice—in that you cannot speak or look or linger without feeling those deadly decisions sticking and tearing at your skin. Nothing is neutral now; nothing is friendly. It's amazing to me to be all tied up and shut up and shut down as a human being in this manner and by this process. People able/disabled/separated/alienated from their own selves and expected still to relate to others as if this disassociation were irrelevant. (White, Mogilka & Slack 1998, 14–15)

How can good work and good workers come out of such an environment? How can such an environment be changed until the emotional and spiritual welfare of the community is considered important? It is largely for this reason that Damrosch concludes that "merely tinkering with requirements in the absence of a larger vision and a sustained commitment to change will have little effect" (1990, 158).

Imagining and defining such a vision demands a great deal from those who would pursue it. It requires

> a loosening of expectations, a willingness to be discomfited, to be prompted, prodded, to think and feel and make [our] own connections. It requires that [we] follow the pull of our narrative without predicting its course. It requires that we all be willing to be uneasy and open to experience, not answers. As we let go of answers and open ourselves to experience, we also open to possibilities—transformative possibilities. (White, Mogilka & Slack 1998, 5)

The following sections are intended simply as starting points for imagining how things might be substantively otherwise—how we might begin to re-envision the academic world that is now so sterile, deadening, and hurtful.

Developing Critical Consciousness

The first step toward imagining a better world will involve a better understanding of the current oppressive system, of the way power is currently used and abused. A critical element here will be for both the oppressors and the oppressed to attain awareness of their relation to each other and of how the inequities of power contribute to an unhealthy environment.

How Might Things Be Otherwise? 153

Some pioneers who have suffered significant backlash for their honesty and courage have nevertheless been working in this area with startling honesty. Acknowledging the extensive privilege and power of the dissertation advisor, faculty supervisor, Thomas Sork, and his student, Valerie Chapman (Chapman & Sork 1999), recently joined by supervisor Shauna Butterwick, have been making public their personal discussions about the role of power in the doctoral advisement system. In their work, they clearly articulate the need for such conversation:

> Addressing issues of power, identity, epistemology, sexuality, oppression and other factors in the student/supervisor relationship is important because they influence the knowledge production/construction process that is so central to graduate education. (Sork, Chapman & Butterwick 1999, 1)

Just so. Discussing such sensitive issues openly will be difficult—and admittedly has been difficult for these researchers—but such honest exploration is imperative to the imagining process. A very first step here, then, might be following the lead these writers have offered and beginning more conversations about

> the role each of us plays in maintaining or resisting the teacher-student relationship and the institutional pressures to reproduce existing power structures. (Sork, Chapman & Butterwick 1999, 1)

Enabling such conversations to take place on a large scale will require more than persuading those who hold power to think about how they use it. It will also involve persuading those who think of themselves as powerless to begin thinking more critically about their situation and about what they can do to help promote an alternative reality.

The task of helping the oppressed in the academy find their voices is going to require the kind of leadership that Sork and a very few others have been providing. A decade ago Tierney (1989b) outlined this need, which has not yet been significantly realized:

> The objective, then, for a critical postmodern democratic politics is to aid in the creating of those voices which have been muffled or silenced by relations of power. This view emphasizes the numerous social relations that exist and investigates how subordination operates and must be challenged if the principles of empowerment and emancipation are

> to work. What are the implications of such a view for our understanding leadership in colleges and universities?
>
> Leadership involves moral action that promotes democracy. Leadership is neither simply a management technique to promote organizational effectiveness, nor is it the accomplishment of a charismatic hero. Leadership is a specific form of empowerment that is intimately connected to the culture of the organization; in effect, leadership provides an active mechanism for achieving an empowered community. Rather than conceive of leadership as something that resides in an individual, the critical theorist views leadership as a reciprocal relationship amongst individuals. (164)

The stance that Tierney advocates is clearly connected to a vision of a more democratic environment where leaders have power not *over* others, but *with* others. He goes on to further define such power, quoting Fay:

> Power in this case is not something which an isolated person can have: it depends on the willingness of the followers as much as the characteristics of the leaders. . . . The powerless are in a fundamental sense not powerless because they share with the powerful the creation of power. It is this implicit power of the oppressed which a critical social theory can tap in order to be a practical instrument of social transformation. . . . [as it] rejects the idea that leadership resides in an office. (164)

That is, we must challenge the notion that power is something invested in institutional leaders, with students cast as official underlings. Instead, we must foster recognition of students as *partners* in what should be a mutually beneficial undertaking. We must undo the sharply demarcated gradations of power in the current hierarchical structure.

Students themselves need to question the assumption that they are entirely powerless, and everyone must question the assumption that all students who leave programs have failed. If the only power students have to end their abuse is to leave the academy, then choosing to leave is an exercise of power, not a failure. The testimony of Dorothea Salo and others makes clear that a conscious decision to end arbitrary abuse is an affirmation of self and of the right to respectful treatment as a human being. More students need to recognize that leaving the academy is one way to deny support to an oppressive system. Of course it is preferable to challenge unacceptable practices, but if the academy refuses to change them, the student always has another choice: to refuse the role of student as it is currently defined.

The concept that the powerless are never wholly without power is one that Rorty (1992) takes great pains to explain, noting that, most often, domination depends on the dominated willingly refraining from using their own power. To make the point most simply, when a student who *could* choose to leave a program elects to stay instead, even in the face of physically and mentally damaging treatment, that student has failed to use his or her own power to stop the suffering. However powerless the student feels, the reality is that he or she could end the experience by exercising what Rorty calls latent power—the unused power to walk out the door.

> Subordinates—the faithful in the Church, the peasants in a feudal system, servants in an aristocracy, students in a university—also have both manifest and latent power.... Hidden within their manifest power is their power to accord cooperation or to subvert the interests of the dominant. The latent power of subordinates is the power of resistance, destruction, noncooperation. This resistance can take two dramatically different forms: without questioning the initial terms and assumptions of the relation, it can attempt to become the dominant party, or it can attempt to transform the character of the relation by denying the assumptions upon which it rests. Because it undermines the terms of the continuing struggle for ascendancy, the second alternative seems more powerful. (3)

Many students, of course, choose the first option—they continue to slog through a program until they complete it, and then they become one of the professors who delight in wielding their unchecked power. Others, like Salo, try to work through channels to challenge faulty assumptions. When that doesn't work, other forms of resisting—both leaving and other more subversive strategies—may still appear.

If it weren't sad, one example of resistance we are familiar with would be funny, indicating the creative extremes students will go to in order to defy the authority and will of the faculty. In Chapter Five, we described an advisor's ambush on a student during a dissertation defense that left the student permanently scarred. Part of the defense outcome was that the student was required to complete extensive and whimsical revisions. Several of her colleagues in the program who had attended the defense were outraged by the abuse they witnessed and determined to try and right at least some of the damage inflicted on their friend.

To save the dissertation writer from a tortuous revision process and from the thoroughly predictable period of depression that would accompany it, the friends decided that they would revise the dissertation for her. A half dozen of them, who had heard all the criticisms and understood the work to be done, gathered one weekend with laptop computers, took a chapter each to revise, and completed the required revisions. The beleaguered dissertation writer was allowed only to talk, not to write, during this time together, and was forbidden to turn in the finished copy for some weeks in order to encourage the advisor to believe she had toiled laboriously over the work. Thus the writer's friends paroled her from the advisor's sentence of additional weeks and hours of useless work. In this way, the students resisted the will of the all-powerful advisor, winning both moral and practical victories on behalf of their oppressed friend.

Only in the most perverse sense, however, is this a positive story—something like jokes about how servants manage to steal from unjust masters. The triumph is hollow because it is momentary, it involves trying to right a wrong with a wrong, and it does nothing to right the essential injustice of the system. Instead, students need to consider a more positive alternative, the one employed by Sork's students: openly questioning and rethinking the way power operates in relationships between people in the academy, and trying to develop alternative visions for those relationships. Such substantive change

> requires and presupposes the power to effect a dramatic reorientation on oneself as well as on others. The more central the issues in a power relation, the more difficult it is for the subordinates to free themselves of their old assumptions, and the more difficult it is for them to change the conditions that reinforce old practices. (Rorty 4)

Developing such critical consciousness among students themselves will be, as Rorty says, a difficult task. It will require more and more experienced voices—more and more Sorks and Chapmans and Butterwicks and Smiths and Hawleys and Tompkins and Satos and Cudes—analyzing their experiences and speaking openly and honestly about them. How successful we are in helping students become participants in the revision of the academic world where they play a crucial role will depend on how successful we are at encouraging and listening to honest voices from every segment of the academy. We will need to be serious and purposeful about doing everything we can to generate what Tierney calls "moral discourse amongst a specific community" (1989a, 165).

Realizing Community

The kind of dialogue just called for will not be easily fostered in the current climate, which currently discourages it by putting so much power into so few hands. Concurrently, then, there is a need to challenge the hierarchical and competitive nature of the status quo. Tompkins aptly characterizes the lived experience of this toxic atmosphere (1996):

> In college I had worked out of aspiration and desire. Though I felt the pressure to get good grades, it was a background pressure, something I had internalized long ago. In graduate school the work turned into something else: a contest to see who could make the best impression on the professor, read the largest number of articles on a topic, come up with the most sophisticated reading of a text. An atmosphere of competitiveness, never spoken or named, permeated the classes and the casual conversation. You could taste it in the coffee and smell it in the corridors. Except for my roommates and a few other people, I never really knew the other students; in class they seemed intimidating, and at parties they made snide comments and knowing remarks that confirmed the impression. . . . I think the truth was that we were all more or less equally at sea, but we didn't want to seem so; so people led with their defenses, everyone afraid of everyone else. (76–77)

Having suffered from this experience, Tompkins herself is easily able to imagine a far more desirable alternative:

> I believe that school should be a safe place, the way home is supposed to be. A place where you belong, where you can grow and express yourself freely, where you know and care for the other people and are known and cared for by them, a place where people come before information and ideas. School needs to comprehend the relationship between the subject matter and the lives of students, between teaching and the lives of teachers, between school and home. (127)

No doubt this characterization will strike many readers as far too idealistic. These more practically oriented readers would do well to consider Tompkins' picture in terms of Melissa Anderson's recent research findings when she surveyed large numbers of graduate students about their experiences (1998):

> An astounding 92 percent of our respondents said that in their department people put their own interests first. Over 70 percent said that faculty were more concerned with the good of the department and that people in their department had to compete for resources.... Students also experienced considerable competition for attention: Roughly half said that in their department students had to compete for faculty time and attention, that a few students got most of the attention and resources, and that faculty members of their department would bend the rules for some but not all.... Clearly, the community that some students find in their department is tempered by considerable competition. (8)

Reports like this suggest that Tompkins' observations are neither exaggerated nor uncommon, and also that her suggestions are firmly grounded in experience. The climate for graduate study must be made safe and far more democratic and ethical than it currently is.

Tierney makes the same point, arguing that concern for humanity and concern for practicality are not mutually exclusive (1987):

> Rather than assuming we exist in an ecological universe, where one's collegiate species must continually adapt, I argue that organizations and environments are socially constructed. I neither advocate nor believe that perception is always reality, yet I give credence to the idea that participants' perceptions of problems, solutions, the environment, and a host of other variables go a long way toward determining the health of the organization.
>
> To be sure, budgets must be balanced, classrooms filled with students, and faculty paid. Yet how shall we perceive that a budget should be balanced, who should sit in classrooms, what students should learn, and who should teach, depends in large part on the organization's enactment of its environment. By working within the framework of organizational culture, administrators learn to consider how change in one programmatic area will affect these other areas. For example, rather than implement an open admissions policy to increase enrollment, the administrator will adopt a mode of strategic analysis that considers how much a change will affect the identity and inner workings of the college for both the short and long term. (71–72)

How Might Things Be Otherwise?

Rather than thinking in hierarchical terms, we need to begin thinking in terms of the institution as a complex community where the health and happiness of every group affects the health and happiness of the whole.

Again, Tompkins has already envisioned such an environment (1996):

> This would mean that the leadership would become self-conscious about the nature of human interaction on the campus, finding a way to involve everybody—undergraduates, secretaries, janitorial staff, administrators, professor at all ranks, part-time faculty, graduate students, visiting scholars. It would mean devoting time and effort to building good relationships. Right now the culture of the research university militates against the quality of life because such concerns are regarded as peripheral to a university's main business. They're perceived as unintellectual, more or less on the level of housekeeping: things to be done, if they're done at all, by someone other than professors, who think that they shouldn't have the responsibility and most probably would not have the aptitude for it, much less the time. This certainly was my own attitude until recently. (193)

If Tompkins has been able to shift her perspective, certainly others are capable of such reconceptualization.

Pursuing the kind of ideal community she envisions is desirable not only because of ideal and ethical concerns, but also because the practical reality is that the current unhappiness and abuse of students has affected both the reputation and the enrollment of the entire graduate school enterprise. Whether concern is for student welfare or for institutional welfare, efforts to pursue a healthier, more collegial and democratic community make sense.

Nourishing the Human Spirit

To speak of health and happiness within a university community, rather than of reputation and income, is in itself a major reorientation of common conceptions of what the academic enterprise is about. And yet, there are even more ephemeral goals worth pursuing. Realizing human potential involves more than mental and physical health. It involves acknowledging that there is also such a thing as spiritual health, and that spirituality is a fully legitimate concern for the academy:

> In contrast [to the natural sciences], human science research is rigorous when it is "strong" or "hard" in a moral and spirited sense. A strong and rigorous human science text distinguishes itself by its courage and resolve to stand up for the uniqueness and significance of the notion to which it has dedicated itself. And what does it mean to stand up for something if one is not prepared to stand out? This means also that a rigorous human science is prepared to be "soft," "soulful," "subtle," and "sensitive" in its effort to bring the range of meanings of life's phenomena our reflective awareness. (Van Manen 1990, 17)

At present, attention to spiritual needs are most often addressed by institutions arranging for students to have some sort of access to a variety of denominational services and perhaps some on-campus religious representative. This is a sort of tokenism, however, since it does little to permeate the climate of the entire community with concern for the spiritual life.

Smith has outlined both the human need for an explicit spirituality and the consequences of ignoring it (1990):

> If history and anthropology have anything to each us, it is that human beings, from the tribe to the traditional cultures of the modern world, have among their most basic needs the need to celebrate, to pay their respects to the invisible powers of the world. We celebrate birthdays, weddings, marriages, anniversaries, even deaths where lives have been fully and fruitfully lived. We mark the holy religious days of all the great faiths of the worlds. It is in our nature to do so. Without the power to celebrate, we are greatly diminished. We suffer a kind of illness of the soul. (208)

This "illness of the soul" is exactly the malady that postmodern writers have been highlighting in recent literature. Kincheloe (1999) discusses "the wounded spirit, the cognitive illness" at length; Johnson (1999) calls for the inclusion of "spiritual intelligence" in post-formal thinking:

> The existence of a spiritual mode of consciousness has been largely obscured by the limited view from the conceptual traps inherent in the modern mind. But to exclude this dimension is to suppress the experience and beliefs of the majority of human beings across cultures and throughout history, including those of original cultures, traditional religious cultures, and indigenous peoples. . . . *spiritual* can be seen as an

aspect of life that is the essence of intelligence, a force animating and connecting all beings and things so that all of life is seen as a sacred whole. (147)

As Kincheloe and Johnson both go to great lengths to detail, we split the human body, mind, and spirit at our peril. When we insist on pretending that elements of the human whole are entirely separate from each other, that some elements (like cognitive processes) are more important than others (like spiritual needs), we ensure our own insufficiency and suffering.

Because we believe spirituality is a critical and badly neglected issue, and since this entire text encourages readers to challenge tradition, we will break with tradition here and risk including an entire section on spirituality from another source. We are well aware that normally, the following would be considered far too long an excerpt to incorporate. But Page Smith is, to our mind, both eloquent and moving in the following extended discussion of spirituality in the academy, and so we include it in its entirety, asking readers to trust our judgment here and to read the entire quotation carefully (1990):

> All right. Let us assume that celebrations and festivals touch us on the deepest levels of our being, exalt us, and heal us, and the absence of them often leaves us isolated and neurotic. What has that to do with higher education? Well, we were talking about the mature person at home in the world, so the connection should be obvious. Students should be reminded of the centrality of celebration and the necessity of festivals throughout human history. More than that, they should experience both. They do, to be sure, have commencement exercises, celebrations of the completion of their college careers, but the black-clothed processions of professors and "graduates" with tedious and repetitious addresses are dispiriting affairs. The closest thing to a festival most campuses can offer are football or basketball "pep rallies." But can festivals simply be introduced into the gray and somber atmosphere of the average institution of higher learning? How about the summer and winter solstices for starters? They already have a respectable history as festivals in many cultures, and they would provide ideal opportunities for emphasizing humankind's dependence on the natural world.
>
> Imagine a campus (perhaps one exists or has existed) where members of the so-called-but-seldom-existing-in-reality academic

> community—faculty, students, and even administrators—gather together to dance and sing and dine! Is that so bizarre, so unacademic, so "emotional" that it cannot even be imagined? How are we to learn to celebrate life and lift our spirits in festivals if we are not taught? How are we to get "in tune" with the world?
>
> How do you think the academic world would react to the notion that it had some responsibilities in such matters? Not the proper business of any respectable university. It may be that at the heart of the primness, the austerity, indeed, of the puritanical temper, of the academy is the uneasy awareness that such rituals contain in themselves the message that "scientific objectivity" does not rule the world, that its hegemony is being challenged, its dominance over our consciousness, our view of ourselves, and our relation to the world. Celebrations and festivals are, after all, primitive and emotional. They are eminently unreasonable, thoroughly irrational. If students want to sing and dance, let them take "Choral Music 101" or "Modern Dance 6B." They can thereby get six units of credit. Or let them sing and dance extracurricularly. Some years ago, on the campus of the University of California, Santa Cruz, the professor in charge of the Western Civilization segment of the World-Civilization course, the college's required "core course" that everyone was expected to take, prevailed on the entire class to sing Handel's *Messiah*. They did not, it must be confessed, sing it very well, but the point was that, in struggling to sing it at all the members of the class gained an insight into the spirit of eighteenth-century Christendom that I believe they could never have gotten in routine classroom exercises. (209–210)

The idea of festivals and celebrations of genuine community as an integral part of university life will strike many readers as absurdly amusing. And yet, some of the institutions where students are happiest have long incorporated precisely such rituals.

At Bryn Mawr College outside Philadelphia, for example, besides special dinners where faculty serve meals to students and then entertain them at extravagant dessert receptions, the community has long held a May Day extravaganza and "step sings"—events where students literally sit outside on building steps singing, with spontaneity and no requirement for talent. There are many precedents, in many places. We can build a spiritual element into our communities. We need only agree on the goal as an imperative.

To return to the thesis detailed early in this chapter: the new world

How Might Things Be Otherwise? 163

we can build will be limited only by our ability to imagine it. We need first to stop assuming we already know what is and isn't possible, to try to banish the deeply ingrained assumptions that keep us wedded to the imperfect now, where the many with lesser power are exploited to maintain the comfort and privilege of the more powerful few.

PARTING THOUGHTS

We have argued that graduate education most frequently operates as an oppressive system overflowing with exploitation and many other abuses of the less powerful. We have provided documentation to support this claim. We have urged reform, and we have outlined possibilities for revision. But what is it, exactly, that we finally ask of the individual reader?

The answer is clearly articulated by Van Manen (1990), who outlines the purpose of the kind of human science we have tried to execute here:

> Phenomenological human science ... sponsors a certain concept of progress ... the progress of humanizing human life and humanizing human institutions to help human beings to become increasingly thoughtful and thus better prepared to act tactfully in situations. (21)

Our purpose has been largely to call attention to the way students experience graduate education, to make clear what the facts and figures about graduate education mean in terms of human struggle, hopes, fears, hardships, disappointments, disillusionment, energy, idealism, and relationships. For all its bricks and mortar, trophies and rankings, no institution exists outside of the human beings who people it. To ignore this fact, as has been the case for far too long, is not only dangerous in practical terms but unconscionable in moral and ethical terms.

We have tried to impose what Van Manen calls an "invitational character" upon our analysis:

> For example, cool water invites us to drink, the sandy beach invites the child to play, an easy chair invites our tired body to sink in it, etc. Similarly, a phenomenological human science text invites a dialogic response from us. (21)

It is this dialogic response, this talking back to our text, that we hope to elicit from the reader at this point.

Are the issues raised here important? Are you concerned about them? Is there a possibility that, consciously or not, you have been supporting an unjust, oppressive system in which graduate students serve well an institution that serves them poorly at best? Will you think seriously and honestly about that, and then take appropriate action to help realize an alternative reality that you can imagine?

If every reader at least ponders these questions and others that will spring from them, we can ask no more of you—or of our work here.

References

AAU. (1998a). *Graduate education in the national interest.* Available: http://www.tulane.edu/~aauGradEDTP.html.

AAU. (1998b). *Report and recommendations.* Available: http://www.tulane.edu/~aau.

AAU. (1999). *Background briefing: Responses to criticisms about graduate education.* Available: http://www.tulane.edu/~aau/Criticisms.html.

AAUP Committee on Graduate Students. (1999). Draft Bill of Rights for Graduate Students. Washington, DC: AAUP.

Adler, N.E. (1976). "Women students." In J. Kutz & R.T. Hartnett (Eds.), *Scholars in the Making* (pp. 197–225). Cambridge, MA: Ballinger.

Airaksinen, T. (1992). The rhetoric of domination. In T. E. Wartenberg (Ed.), *Rethinking power* (pp. 102–120). Albany: SUNY Press.

Anderson, M. (1996). *Impostors in the temple: A blueprint for improving higher education in America.* Stanford: Hoover Institution Press.

Anderson, M. S. (Ed.). (1998). *The experience of being in graduate school: An exploration.* San Francisco: Jossey-Bass.

Astin, A. (1982). *Minorities in American higher education: Recent trends, current prospects and recommendations.* San Francisco: Jossey-Bass.

Austin, A. (1990). Faculty cultures, faculty values. *New Directions for Institutional Research, 68,* 61–95.

Baird, L. (1990). The personal and professional development of graduate and professional school students. In J. C. Smart (Ed.), *Higher education: Handbook of theory and research* (Vol. 6,). New York: Agaton Press.

Baird, L. (Ed.). (1993a). *Increasing graduate student retainment and degree attainment.* San Francisco: Jossey-Bass.

Baird, L. (1993b). Studying graduate student retention and degree attainment: Resources for researchers. *New Directions for Institutional Research, 80*, 81–90.

Baird, L. (1996). Documenting student outcomes in graduate and professional programs. *New Directions in Institutional Research, 90*, 77–87.

Barnett, S. (1982). New brains for old: The impact of emotional and physical stress during the Ph.D. period. In S. Vartuli (Ed.), *The Ph.D. experience: A woman's point of view* (pp. 61–69). New York: Praeger.

Berelson, G. (1960). *Graduate education in the United States.* New York: McGraw-Hill.

Bolig, R.A. (1982). The ambivalent decision. In Vartuli, S. (Ed.), *The Ph.D. experience: A woman's point of view* (pp. 15–26). New York: Praeger.

Boufis, C. (1990). *Strange bedfellows: Does academic life lead to divorce?* [On line serial]. Salon Magazine. Available: http://www.salonmagazine.com/it/feature/1990/03/24/feature.html.

Bowen, W., & Rudenstine, N. (1992). *In pursuit of the Ph.D.* Princeton: Princeton University Press.

Browning, Robert. Andrea del Sarto. In *Oxford Dictionary of Quotations.* London: Oxford University Press.

Caplan, P. (1994). *Lifting a ton of feathers: A woman's guide to surviving in the academic world.* Toronto: Toronto University Press.

Chaffee, E., & Tierney, W. (1998). *Collegiate culture and leadership strategies.* New York: ACE-Oryx.

Chapman, V., & Sork, T. J. (1999, April). *Confessing regulation or telling secrets? Opening up the conversation on graduate supervision.* Paper presented at the Annual Meeting of the American Educational Research Association, Montreal.

Cherryholmes, C. (1988). *Power and criticism: Poststructural investigations in education.* New York: Teachers College Press.

Clark, B.R. (1985). Listening to the professoriate. *Change, 17*(5), 36–43.

Conrad, T., & Eagan, D. (1989). The prestige game in American higher education. *Thought and Action, 5*(1), 5–16.

Cude, W. (1988). *The Ph.D. trap.* West Bay, Nova Scotia: Medicine Label Press.

Damrosch, D. (1995). *We scholars: Changing the culture of the university.* Cambridge: Harvard University Press.

Dooley-Dickey, K., & Satcher, J. (1991). Doctoral disorder of adulthood. *Journal of Mental Health Counseling, 33*(4), 486–491.

Evans, N. J., & Wall, V. A. (Eds.). (1991). *Beyond tolerance: Gays, lesbians and bisexuals on campus.* Alexandria, VA: American College Personnel Association.

Fischer, F. (1985). Critical evaluation of public policy: A methodological case study. In J. Forester (Ed.), *Critical theory and public life* (pp. 231–257). Cambridge, MA: MIT Press.

Freire, P. (1981). *Pedagogy of the oppressed* (Myra Berman Ramos, Trans.). New York: Continuum.
Freire, P. (1985). *The Politics of education: Culture, power and liberation* (Donaldo Macedo, Trans.). Wilton, CT: Bergin & Garvey.
Graham, A., & Morse, R. (1999). *How we rank graduate schools* [On-line]. U.S. News & World Report. Available: http://www.usnews.com/usnews/edu/beyondgradrank/gbrank.htm.
Grassmuck, K. (1991, May 15). What happened at Standord: Key mistakes at critical times in a battle with the government over research costs. *Chronicle of Higher Education*, pp. A25–27.
Guarasci, R., & Cornwell, G. (1997). Liberal education as intercultural practice: Citizenship in a diverse democracy. In R. Guarasci & G. Cornwell (Eds.), *Democratic education in an age of difference* (pp. 159–170). San Francisco: Jossey-Bass.
Hall, S. (1998, November 29). Lethal chemistry at Harvard. *New York Times Magazine, 120,* 6.
Hanson, T. (1992). *The ABD Phenomenon: The "at risk" population in higher education and the discipline of communication.* Paper presented at the Speech Communication Association, Chicago, IL.
Hawley, P. (1993). *Being bright is not enough.* Springfield IL: Charles C. Thomas.
Heinrich, K. (1995). Doctoral advisement relationships between women. *Journal of Higher Education, 66*(4), 447–469.
Johnson, A. N. (1999). Post-formal thinking, spiritual intelligence and the paradox of the developmental journey. In J. L. Kincheloe, S. Steinberg, & P. H. Hinchey (Eds.), *The post-formal reader: Cognition and education* (pp. 146–173). New York: Falmer Press.
Kaplan. (1999a). *GRE 1999–2000.* New York: Kaplan.
Kaplan. (1999b). *Kaplan Newsweek graduate school admissions advisor.* New York: Simon & Schuster.
Kerlin, B. A. (1997). *Breaking the silence: Toward a theory of women's doctoral persistence.* Unpublished dissertation, University of Victoria, British Columbia.
Kerlin, B. A. S. (1995a). *Hidden rules, secret agenda: Challenges facing contemporary women doctoral students.* Paper presented at the American Educational Research Association, San Francisco, CA.
Kerlin, S. P. (1995b). Pursuit of the Ph.D.: "Survival of the fittest," or is it time for a new approach? *Educational Policy Analysis Archives.* Available: http://olam.ed.asu.edu/epaa/v3n16.html.
Kerlin, S. P., & Smith, B. (1994). *Electrifying stories: Virtual research communities in graduate education.* Paper presented at the Pacific Northwest Association for Institutional Research and Planning, Portland, OR.

Kincheloe, J. L. (1999). Trouble ahead, trouble behind: Grounding the post-formal critique of educational psychology. In J. L. Kincheloe, S. Steinberg, & P. H. Hinchey (Eds.), *The post-formal reader: Cognition and education* (pp. 4–54). New York: Falmer Press.

Koeske, G., & Koeske, R. D. (1991). Student "burnout" as a mediator of the stress-outcome relationship. *Research in Higher Education, 32*(4), 415–31.

LaPidus, J. B. (1998). If we want things to stay as they are, things will have to change. In M. S. Anderson (Ed.), *The experience of being in graduate school: An exploration* (pp. 95–102). San Francisco: Jossey-Bass.

Latimer, J. (Ed.). (1999). *Graduate schools in the U.S.* New York: Peterson's.

Leatherman, C. (1996, November 29). Faculty and graduate student strife over job issues flares on many campuses. *Chronicle of Higher Education*, pp. A12–14.

Leatherman, C. (1998). *Teaching assistants plan showdown over unionization* [on-line]. Available: http://www.chronicle.com/colloquy/98/ta/background.

Levstik, L. S. (1982). The impossible dream: The Ph.D., marriage and the family. In S. Vartuli (Ed.), *The Ph.D. experience: A woman's point of view*. New York: Praeger.

Lightman, A., & Brawer, R. (1990). *Origins: The lives and worlds of modern cosmologists*. Cambridge, MA: Harvard University Press.

Lipschutz, S. (1993). Enhancing success in doctoral education: From policy to practice. In L. Baird (Ed.), *Increasing graduate student retention and degree attainment: New directions for institutional research*. San Francisco: Jossey-Bass.

McConnell, M. A. (1982). High noon: Surviving the comprehensive exams. In S. Vartuli (Ed.), *The Ph.D. experience: A woman's point of view*. New York: Praeger.

Mitchell, L. (1996). *The ultimate grad school survival guide: Getting in, getting money, exams and classes, the profs, the thesis/dissertation*. New York: Peterson's Guides.

Mohamadi, A. (1998). *Yale Daily News guide to fellowships and grants*. New York: Kaplan.

NRC. (1996). *Research-doctorate programs in the United States: Continuity and change*. Washington, D.C.: National Academic Press.

Pacchioli, D. (1998). *Bringing in the best* [on-line]. Research/Penn State. Available: http://www.research.psu.edu/rps/sep98/editor.

Peterson's. (1998). *Peterson's compact guide: Graduate studies in education 1999*. New York: Peterson's Guides.

Quinnan, T. W. (1997). *Adult students "at-risk": Culture bias in higher education*. Westport, CT: Bergin & Garvey.

References

Salo, D. (1999). *A tale of graduate school burnout*. Available: http://www.terracom.net/~dorothea/gradsch.

Sanders, J., Koch, J., & Urso, J. (1997). *Gender equity*. Mahwah, NJ: Lawrence Erlbaum.

Schied, F. (1995). *"How did humans become resources anyway?": HRD and the politics of learning in the workplace*. Paper presented at the Adult Education Research Conference, University of Alberta, Edmonton.

Smith, P. (1990). *Killing the spirit: Higher education in America*. New York: Viking.

Sork, T., Chapman, V., & Butterwick, S. (1999). *She said, he said, they said: High drama in the continuing saga of graduate student supervision*. Paper presented at the Canadian Association for the Study of Adult Education, Sherbrooke, Quebec.

State University of New York at Buffalo. Available: http://www.grad.buffalo.edu/pros-stud/overview.htm.

Stelzer, R. (1997). *How to write a winning personal statement for graduate and professional school*. New York: Peterson's Guides.

Sternberg, D. (1981). *How to complete and survive a doctoral dissertation*. New York: St. Martin's Press.

Thomas, C. T. (1999). *Questions to ask before hitting the rough road to graduate school*. Available: http://www.petersons.com/graduate/transitions2.

Tierney, W. G. (1987). Facts and constructs: Defining reality in higher education organizations. *Review of Higher Education, 11*(1), 61–73.

Tierney, W. G. (1989a). Advancing democracy: A critical interpretation of leadership. *Peabody Journal of Education, 66*(3), 157–175.

Tierney, W. G. (1989b). Cultural politics and the curriculum in postsecondary education. *Journal of Education, 171*(3), 72–88.

Tierney, W. G. (1991). Academic work and institutional culture: Constructing knowledge. *Review of Higher Education, 14*(2), 199–216.

Tierney, W. G. (1992). Cultural leadership and the search for commlunity. *Liberal Education, 7*(5), 16–21.

Tinto, V. (1993). *Leaving college: Rethinking the causes and cures of student attrition*. (2nd ed.). Chicago: University of Chicago Press.

Tokarczyk, M., & Fay, E. (Eds.). (1993). *Working-class women in the academy: Laborers in the knowledge factory*. Amherst, MA: University of Massachusetts Press.

Tompkins, J. (1996). *A life in school: What the teacher learned*. Reading, MA: Addison-Wesley.

Triggle, D. (1996). *The future ain't what it used to be or the university as the Donner party*. Available: http://www.grad.buffalo.edu/general/reports/donner.htm.

Triggle, D. (1997). *Considerest not the beam that is in thine own eye?* Available: http://www.grad.buffalo.edu/general/reports/beam.htm.

Turner, C., & Thompson, J. (1993). Socializing women doctoral students: Minority and majority experiences. *Review of Higher Education, 16*(3), 355–370.

University of Alabama at Birmingham. Available: http://main.vab.edu/show.asp?durki-2414.

Vartuli, S. (Ed.). (1982). *The Ph.D. experience: A woman's point of view.* New York: Praeger.

Wartenberg, T. E. (Ed.). (1992). *Rethinking power.* Albany, NY: SUNY Press.

Weiland, S. (1998). Grand possibilities and perilous business: Academic autobiographers on graduate education. In M. S. Anderson (Ed.), *The experience of being in graduate school* (pp. 15–28). San Francisco: Jossey-Bass.

Willie, C.V., Grady, M.K., & Hope, R.O. (1991). *African Americans and the doctoral experience: Implications for policy.* New York: Teachers College Press.

Wilshire, B. (1990). *The moral collapse of the university: Professionalism, purity, and alienation.* Albany, NY: SUNY Press.

Young, I. (1992). Five faces of oppression. In T. E. Wartenberg (Ed.), *Rethinking power* (pp. 174–195). Albany, NY: SUNY Press.

Ziolkowski, T. (1990). The Ph. D. squid. *American Scholar, 59,* 177–95.

Index

AAU, 4
   Graduate Education in the National Interest, 7–9
   Report and Recommendations, 4–13
Airaksinen, 27–28
Anderson, Martin, 48–49, 57–58, 72, 73, 109
Anderson, Melissa, 13, 157–158
Astin, 64–65
Attrition, 3
Austin, 47, 48, 52, 53, 55, 58, 59, 60, 61

Baird, 103, 139
Bowen and Rudenstine, 3, 13, 71, 73–74, 93, 94, 101, 137–138, 139, 140, 141–142, 145–146

Chaffee and Tierney, 45, 52
Cherryholmes, 21
Cognitive illness, 160–161
Commercial materials, 32–35
Community, cultivating, 157–159
Conrad and Eagen, 53–54

Constructed consciousness, 25, 26–35, 38–39
Critical consciousness, 135, 152–157
Critical theory, 20–23, 135–137
Cude, 1
Culture (*see also* Student experience)
   academic types of, 47–48
   of disciplines, 59–61
   of higher education, 48–51
   of institutional type, 51–54
   and oppression, 63–65
   organizational, 45–46
   of the professoriate, 54–55

Damrosch, 90–91, 136, 138, 143, 147, 151
Dissertation
   advising, 98–104
   committees and defenses, 104–107
   proposed reforms, 143–143, 147–149
   as reified practice, 89–93
   topics, 94–98

171

Ethics, 13, 55–58, 73
Evans and Wall, 84

Faculty advising, 98–104
   disincentives for, 60
   and dissertations, 104–107
   problems with, 12, 77
   reform of, 143–146, 152–153
Freire, 21, 22, 39, 66

Guarsci and Cornwell, 88
Golde, 55–56
Graham and Morse, 28, 29

Hanson, 71, 90, 138, 148–149
Hawley, 18, 52–53, 64, 69, 70, 95, 99, 100, 103, 143, 151
Hegemony, 22, 25, 35–39
Heinrich, 98, 99, 104

Institutional capital, 23
   faculty as, 30, 53–54, 100
   graduate students as, 10–11, 29–30, 75–76
   reputation as, 28–32
Institutional expectations, 146–150

Johnson, 160–161

Kerlin, Bobbi, 14–15, 16–18
Kerlin, Scott, 14–16

LaPidus, 141
Lipschutz, 138

Mitchell, 33–34

Oppression (*see also* Critical theory)
   defined, 21
   forms of, 65–69
   of lesbian and gay students, 82–87, 88, 97–98
   of older students, 78–82, 88
   of students of color, 73–78, 88
   of women, 69–73, 76–78, 878, 96–97
   of working class students, 87–88

Pacchioli, 30
Preparing Future Faculty program, 5, 141

Quinnan, 63, 64, 78, 81, 82

Reform
   call for support of, 163–164
   philosophical areas of, 150–163
   practical areas of, 137–150
      funding, 139–141
      accountability, 141–143
      advising and mentoring, 143–146
   of institutional expectations, 146–150
      for people, 149–150
      for programs, 146–149
Reification, 25, 40–43, 89–93, 136
Rorty, 46, 155, 156

Salo, 19, 41–43
Sexual harassment, 72–73
Schied, 9
Silence, 20, 22, 71, 153–157
Situated power, 37–38
Smith, 59, 89, 92, 93, 136, 138, 149, 160, 161–162
Sork, Chapman, and Butterwick, 103, 153

Index

Sowinska, 88
Spirituality, 159–163
Student experience
   and institutional culture,
      61–62
   narratives of, 109–134
   research on, 13–19
Survival, 1–2, 33–35, 61–62

Tierney, 63, 153–154, 158
Time-to-degree, 2, 95–96, 142, 146, 147, 150
Tokarcyk and Fay, 71, 145
Tompkins, 2, 45, 107, 157, 159
Triggle, 25, 43
Turner and Thompson, 70, 71, 76

Van Manen, 135, 160, 163
Violence
   defined, 68
   students as perpetrators, 1–2
   students as victims, 77, 83–85

Wartenburg, 37–38, 39
Weiland, 36, 79, 87
White, Mogilka and Slack, 152
Willie, Grady, and Hope, 74–75, 144

Young, 65, 67, 68

Ziolkowski, 92, 95, 96, 138, 147–148, 150

For Product Safety Concerns and Information please contact our EU representative GPSR@taylorandfrancis.com
Taylor & Francis Verlag GmbH, Kaufingerstraße 24, 80331 München, Germany